# PUNK DRUNK

---

## AN ETHAN WARES SKATEBOARD SERIES
BOOK 4

## MARK MAPSTONE

# 1

## UP IN SMOKE

It was a cold and cloudy afternoon when Ethan slotted a spanner over his kingpin and spun it into a frictionless vortex. 'It doesn't fit.' He handed it back to Mike. 'You got any others?' He couldn't bash the kid, but what skater carries a 15mm? A wobble he could handle, but when things reach a Daewon level it's time to tighten up the slack.

Today's meet up was at the newly built plaza, that consisted of a foot high square block around a tree and nearly two on the far side. Brand new smooth concrete slabs covered the floor, and as soon as the fences came down, the skaters were all over it. The renovation of the old cobble-stone square of infinite insurance claims had been funded by a wealthy entrepreneur who recently moved into the area. The newspaper ink was still gossipy with the pledge to employ, invest, and expand operations of their honey production business. As far as the skaters were concerned, the real ball-ache came from the purchase of the Ubley Estate, as they had earmarked one of the barns for a winter indoor mini-ramp. That idea had now gone the way of the demolition in progress across the road.

A huge JCB bucket pulled a wall over from twenty feet up, which sent bricks and mortar crashing down into a pile of dust.

Mike's friend Kyle arrived and was immediately ribbed for wearing a pair of trousers several sizes too big everywhere except the legs. The kid kicked away their comments like a boss. Still, this was a fashion faux pas Ethan couldn't comprehend.

The bottoms were wide like the kids' influences and the turn-ups deep to match his bank balance.

Another sucker.

More rubble crashed from the building works.

'What do you think Ethe?' Mike pointed out Kyle's trousers. '£120.'

'They'd need to pay me that to wear them.'

'Are you going to that Nike event?' Mike asked. A premiere was happening in Bristol and everyone who was anyone was invited, which meant, as Ethan was the only anyone they knew, he must have had an offer.

'No chance,' he said. 'Screw Nike.'

'Can I have your invite?' Mike was ready for the rebuttal. His friends quickly followed and began bickering amongst themselves for the ticket as if it would manifest out of Ethan's pocket into their hands.

'It doesn't work like that. The ticket has my name on it. Besides, I didn't accept it.'

'Why not?' Fancy Trousers asked. 'I heard Nyjah was going to be there.' His friends scoffed at the unlikely appearance, but still, the kid hugged that rumour like a true fan. 'I'm going anyway,' he said. 'I just want to see who turns up and maybe get something autographed.'

'Imagine being on Nike,' another kid said. They all replied in unison at how dope it would be.

The digger bucket jammed itself into a wall and clanked backwards and forwards trying to dislodge something steel reinforced.

'How about I get my ticket changed to the name of the first person who lands a hardflip?'

'None of us can hardflip,' Mike said. But that didn't stop Fancy Trousers getting on his board to try it. Everyone else joined him, and eventually, Mike gave in and tried as well. Ethan left the grommets to it and took a roll around the ledges.

Too many people at the plaza in Fluro jackets was never a good sign. The workers who carried concrete dust in their boot grooves and under their fingernails were welcome; they had a job to do and could easily be ignored, but everyone carrying a clipboard was a problem. One such council officer took photos, measured areas, and noted issues. Ethan kept his distance, but not the younger skaters. A loose board from a hard-flip session rolled out and the officer politely stepped aside to let the kid retrieve it. Fancy Trousers gave up his hard-flip attempts first and started a manual roll train across the ledge towards the officer. Not a good move. Soon a board headed straight for the man's Achilles tendons again.

'Here's a bad slab.' Ethan guided the man away from the kids. The officer stood on the slab and tried to rock it with his weight. 'It's within our tolerances.'

'The edge is higher than the others.' Ethan pointed at the lip. 'These wheels find all imperfections.' But the officer stressed it wasn't an issue.

A van towing a mini digger pulled up onto the curb near the end of the high ledge. Three workmen got out.

'Have you got more work planned?' Ethan nodded in the workmen's direction.

'Not by us. They must be contractors working on the pelican crossing.'

The team lifted out blocks from the back of the trailer. The type designed to allow the blind to feel their way to the curb. The worst kind.

James from N27 research pulled up in a branded car.

Mike saw him first. 'Is that the location? Where are you going?' Mike asked.

'No idea,' Ethan replied. 'You asked me that last time and the answer is still the same.'

'I still don't get why they won't tell you.'

'I don't see the point in keeping it quiet either, but the marketing team want it all hush-hush.'

'Why? We'd still watch it,' Mike said, 'It'll probably make it better because we'd tell everyone.'

James didn't have a folder in his hands. 'I don't think you'll need a full briefing this time. You're skating that.' He pointed across the street to a six-stair handrail outside the Hives Honey shop.

'You're kidding?' People skated that rail all the time, but it was a one-hit-wonder cut off by the road and very little other options for lines. 'We've got a whole plaza here and they pick the Hives retail rail? How are people supposed to get excited?'

James shrugged. 'You'll have to get creative. And make it good because your stats have been slipping. Between you and me, Marketing is already dreaming up new ideas.'

'As long as they stick to adverts and whatever else they do. I don't want them anywhere near me.'

During Ethan's first week at N27, he was asked to come up with a hundred riding locations to pitch to management for the series. A hundred? In a small town like Ubley. That was asking a lot. The first ten were a breeze, and it took him another twenty-four hours to come up with another ten. Days passed getting creative to push the list to forty. The final squeeze involved searching maps to bring the list to fifty. This included the slightest bump-gap, buckled tarmac, couple of steps, and any random concrete slope which included the dull Hives rail. The results all ended up in a presentation which looked good on a big screen but was eighty per cent bullshit. He was promised most wouldn't make the final list. That was the first lie of many.

Ethan skated off, annoyed. James hung about for a bit wondering if he was returning for a conversation or questions until he figured he wasn't and left.

The workmen were the more immediate problem as they set down their tools right in front of the pelican crossing, blocking the landing of the big ledge. A few of the kids had already complained, but the workers didn't care. The session would be ruined once those slabs were set. Luckily, their arrival meant his spanner options increased. They were happy to open the lid of the toolbox and let him find the right size for his trucks. Whilst the workers were occupied, Ethan took the fattest spanner he could find and flipped the lid of the mini digger's battery compartment. A large spark jumped from the unit as he dropped it on top of the terminals. He shut the lid and finished tightening his trucks, then skated off to the other side of the plaza.

He ollied into a backside 50-50 and hopped out, then carved around to the next ledge and bonked a quick little crook off the corner. He no-complied around to fakie and half-cab flipped himself straight again and tre-flipped a traffic cone on its side. The workers shooed the kids away and a brief mouthy exchange followed. It was a bad move, but understandable. They could see what Ethan could: the men were wrecking the day, the roll, and the ledge.

One of the workers unhooked the back of the trailer and pulled out the ramps for the mini digger. It was going to be an interesting few minutes. As soon as they turned the ignition, a crack of electricity popped and a plume of burnt plastic smoke wafted out of the cab. The electrics had completely blown. Two other workmen walked around to the cab and waved the smoke from their face. They tried the ignition again, but it was dead. Within minutes of arriving, they started lifting the blocks back into the trailer.

'They're leaving?' Mike said.

'It looks like you'll be having a good session, after all.'

**2**

## A TICKETING ISSUE

The annual water festival cruise of over 250 boats, barges, and yachts brought thousands of people into the area for the weekend. Residents usually moaned about parking and litter, whilst applying for temporary trading licenses to flog stuff at extortionate prices to gullible punters. A party would roll late into Saturday evening and start back up at 11 am on Sunday. It was a great spot for a leisurely wander, though that small joy came with a hefty price tag at the turnstiles to keep out the undesirables.

The skaters either hung around to hook up with people or got the hell out of the area for a couple of days.

Ethan sat by the waterfront waiting for his brother. Heston's taxi was fighting through traffic with a disability badge slapped on the dashboard giving them preferential treatment through the diversions.

Queues of people shuffled and bumped slowly past him towards the market stall tat. It gave him some time to reflect on the retail rail, and with-it Private Joel Reeds fine words from the Leisure Centre. *Break a habit*, he said. *If things keep going wrong, it was probably happening for a reason. Change something.* This annoyed him at the time and had niggled him ever since. Mostly because he wasn't sure what to do exactly. Reed seemed to know the answer but wouldn't say.

Across from the crowds, a couple chatted to friends, and one old man enthusiastically rubbed the belly of a Golden Retriever. When he stopped and returned to the conversation, it sat at its owner's feet and waited patiently for a treat. He sure got one too, along with a pat on the head and a *good boy*. He watched the group walk through the crowds a little more before stopping. Again, the dog sat and looked up at the owner who instinctively gave it another treat. Two treats in thirty seconds. That *good boy* was well-trained, or maybe the owners were? Perhaps that's what Joel Reed meant: N27 had him well-trained too.

Eventually, the click of Heston's crutches crept up from behind as his taxi pulled away from the curb.

'I'm regretting this now.' Ethan looked at the crowds funnelling alongside the barriers queuing to get inside. 'It's £25 a ticket.'

'It gets more expensive every year.'

'Let's blag it.'

The brothers joined the queue shuffling slowly towards the security guards who diligently checked each ticket. They weren't real security guards though. Just dumb hired hands in a jacket, paid for one weekend only to follow orders. Most of them just wanted to get through the minimum wage day and go home. As Heston hobbled forwards, people realised he was on crutches and gave him extra room. Once at the front of the queue, the guard's tone changed from passive-aggressive monotony to one of compassion, empathy, and a friendly smile.

'There's been a mix-up with the ticketing,' Heston said. 'Our charity booked tickets ahead of time, but we've got to go inside to collect them. The woman at the booth told us to speak to you about letting us through.'

Before the security guard could even take a breath, Ethan stepped forward.

'I'm with him,' he said. 'His medical support. This has all been cleared with head office. Dave. You know, Dave? Dave spoke to us and told Pat. Pat from Tickets. She told us to go on through. She's not there now, but it's all been OK'd.'

Heston began walking on and Ethan supported him in making a few steps, asking for space.

The security guard looked over towards the woman at the booth, he didn't even know what her name was. It could've been Pat and who the hell was Dave? 'Sorry, I can't just let you through,' he said. 'I need to check with my superiors.'

'Great. Check,' Heston said. 'But we will have collected our bands before you've got an answer.'

The guards face twitched with decisions, as he looked back at the queue behind them, remembered he had to keep the crowds moving.

'I told you it's all been cleared up,' Ethan moved closer to the guard. 'Besides, I've got to get this man to his medication. He could collapse here at any minute.'

The guard grabbed the bar and the turnstile stopped abruptly.

'I can't let you in if you don't have a ticket.'

A voice in the crowd realised what was happening. 'They're trying to get in without tickets.'

Ethan gently pushed the guard back. 'That contract you signed to do this job, had a lot of words in it, which you clearly haven't read. You can't stop a man from having their medication. You'll be sued and never work again. It's just not worth it.'

But the guard stood firm, and another voice

whipped up the crowd. 'They're trying to get in without tickets.'

Things were beginning to escalate, and more questions were just going to create more checks and less chance of getting in. That guard stiffened with all the rules stuffed in his head. The brothers thought they'd cut their losses and get out of the queue before things got nasty. Besides, there was always another way in.

Music hung in the air along with the irritating scent of spicy food.

'How's the counselling going?' Heston asked.

'Not too bad. She's pretty good. I've looked her up online and well, you wouldn't believe it, but she's been a celebrity therapist for years. Famous ones, too.'

'What does that matter?'

Ethan wasn't sure how to answer that, but he was just happier being in the hands of someone experienced. For so long he felt alone, but now he felt like he had someone he could talk to. 'She's been getting me to think about what happened and look at it a different way. A huge weight has lifted off my shoulders. I think you should see her too.'

'I can't face going through all of that again,' Heston said. 'You stick with it. You need it more than meme.'

At the back of the festival stallholders had unhooked a section of fencing and were busy unloading supplies of t-shirts, frozen fish, stacks of paper cups, and bottled water to keep the hungry mouths fed and tills ringing up with cash. The brothers edged closer to the fencing gap and checked for any sign of security. No one was covering the back. Maybe they assumed that all the law-abiding citizens would funnel their way through the queues to the main entrance, without thinking that anyone else would have the balls to blend in with the stallholders. Big mistake. The stallholders couldn't even care who was hanging around the back as long as they weren't stealing stuff. It was too easy. The brothers waited for another stall-holder to walk through with a stack of cups in his hands and then just followed him in. No-one batted an eyelid.

Once inside, they made their way out into the main seating area. It was only eleven in the morning but many of the seats were already taken, except one bench which they quickly took.


'You know I've got the retail rail location this week?'

Heston nodded.

Ethan shook his head. 'Whoever's picking these, is out to get me.'

'How?'

'Gut feeling.' Ethan grabbed his stomach and gave it a shake. 'I'm serious though. Who picked it?'

Heston looked puzzled and shrugged. 'I don't know. I've been away for a week.'

Ethan leant back a little, sighed, and pushed his hands deep into his pockets. 'I'm just getting this weird feeling about N27.'

'Like what?'

'Like I'm caught in a catch-22. Getting some spot each week, and not even a good one, skating my ass off, nearly dying in the process, then something…' Ethan took a moment and tried to think of what he was trying to say. 'Something happens which shouldn't. I mean. Am I just unlucky? The edits are good, but the stats are falling, and Ricard's edits seem to be doing better. I thought it was Flint, messing with me, but now she's out of the department, I thought it would get better.'

'What are you going on about?'

Ethan didn't know exactly. 'Maybe, I should change it?'

'Change what? The rail? You can't,' Heston said. 'It's scheduled.'

'Remember in the Girl video with the obstacles? I was thinking, why don't I do the same thing to the retail rail?'

'Which Girl video you talking about?'

'Fully Flared.'

'They blew up the obstacles.'

## 3

## WARNED OFF

'I could do that. Blow up the rail just like they did.' Ethan's pulse increased just at the thought of grinding the rail whilst it exploded beneath him.

'Don't be stupid,' Heston laughed. 'N27 would never go with it and you're an idiot for thinking they would. How exactly are you going to do it? You don't know anything about pyrotechnics, then there's the insurance.'

'I'm not going to need insurance.'

'Of course, you are.' Heston couldn't believe what he was hearing. 'N27 has to pay a huge premium as it is. Who knows what it'll cost to cover a high public risk like that. They'll never go for it.'

'You think it's stupid? I mean, it would be amazing right? No-one will expect it.'

'Trust me, bro. Even if there was a microscopic chance of pulling this off, you could lose your contract. Have you ever thought about that? They're just looking for a reason to hang you out to dry. They'd fire you.'

Ethan sat back and thought about all the corporate bullshit he had to deal with, and his excitement started to dissipate as the reality of pulling the stunt off dawned on him.

Heston left to pee, which gave Ethan some time to think. Maybe he could come up with a new idea, one which was just as exciting but less dangerous. Ricards edits were starting to get to him. His Line-life nonsense shouldn't even be working, but for some reason, the kids liked it. He didn't want to think about it any more. It was making his brain hurt. Not only that but the music changed from 80s reggae to 80s pop.

Suddenly he was aware of someone beside him. It was the security guard from the gate.

'You again,' the guard said. 'I didn't let you in. Where's your band?'

Ethan looked over to the toilets for any sign of Heston. He had a thought that this goon might just be doing his job, but had he been tested? It looked increasingly likely that a problem was going to appear. Problems were something Ethan had had enough of lately.

'My brothers got it. He'll be back in a minute.'

'If you don't have a band then you need to leave.' The security guard stepped back. 'Come on, or get out now.' The guard took out his radio and called for backup. It was clear that he wasn't going to let it drop.

A drained feeling of the *same old bullshit* ran through Ethan's body. 'Haven't you got anything else to do? It's not like you get paid more if you kick people out. This is supposed to be a happy festival, so let us fest and be happy.'

'What's going on?' Heston asked.

'This idiot is causing trouble.' Ethan pointed at the guard.

'Right, get out!' The guard tried to lift Ethan out of his seat.

'Get off me.' He shrugged the guard away. Heston pushed the end of his crutch into the guard, but he grabbed it.

Heston swung the other crutch up and thumped the guard in the ribcage.

At that point, all actions blurred into one.

The guard batted the crutches away and grabbed Ethan by his arms to pull him up out of his seat. Ethan twisted out of that grab, stepped aside, and dropped the guard with a kick to the back of the knee. As more guards arrived, they saw Ethan wrestling with the guard in a headlock. He still had a fistful of Heston's shirt and all three were tangled up on the ground. This immediately attracted attention from the other festivalgoers, who came to the brothers' defence. They didn't care whether they had tickets or not, they saw bullies fighting a young man on crutches. The guards were surrounded and heavily outnumbered, trying to justify their actions and restrain the fighting pair. Eventually, a senior member of the security team arrived, and upon seeing the distress caused, calmed the situation down.

'Let them go. They can stay.'

As the guards were pulled away back to their posts, the senior member, helped Heston off the ground.

'Please accept our apologies.' The man made sure everyone could hear him, then quietly said, 'We know you don't have tickets, but we're prepared to let it go for now. If you cause any more trouble, you will be removed.' He spoke through a large smile and then turned to the crowd again. 'I've just made sure everyone is OK. There's nothing to see here. Please continue with your day.'

The tension dissipated and allowed the vibrant sensory onslaught of the festival to pull the crowd's attention back towards the stalls. Neither of them were hurt. Some clothing needed straightening and their hands needed wiping, but otherwise, they let it pass, and joked about the hideous tie-dye T-shirts for sale on a nearby stall.

Some roadies came on stage to soundcheck the band's equipment and one of the guitarists changed a broken string on a Les Paul. A vegan food stall-holder asked if they wanted to [...] but it wasn't long before Ethan [...] thinking about his edit for the week.

'Something is against me, every week.'

'Let it go,' Heston said.

'I'm going to do what Joel Reed said, I'm going to lay a trap.'

'Who?'

'The guy from the leisure centre.'

'He told to you to lay a trap?'

'Not exactly, but it seemed to work for him.'

'Just hold up,' Heston said. 'You've got a good job, it might not be the best company, but at least you've got it. You're over-thinking all this. I know you and I know why you're doing it.'

'It's because I've got nothing else.'

'No. It's not,' Heston insisted. 'You've got everything you need. A job, exposure, and God knows how much you love that! The kids don't hate you, unlike your old crew, who still don't want anything to do with you, by the way.'

'Yeah, so about that…'

'Shut up and listen for once. Forget trying to get back in with them. They'll come round eventually. Just keep doing what you're doing.'

A moment of silence allowed Ethan to think about his brother's advice. They always looked after each other. Sticking together through the thick and thin of their childhood. Heston cared for him more didn't have to. Ethan

.t,' Ethan said. 'But it
ight?'
head and kept walking.
re.'

The moment Loretta opened the door to her new practice, the stench of a vanilla fragrance plugin hit him. His nose itched, and he knew those droplets would cling to his skin like the lemon scent of a public toilet. He coughed, swallowed hard, and made his way to the chair in the middle of the room.

'This is the new place. It's much better than the old one.' Loretta hung her coat on a hook and quickly checked her emails. 'More space and light, and a better view of the city.'

Ethan looked around the room for that little spitting devil, first up high, and then around the skirting boards. It was on the far side of the room beneath a wall of certificates. They all looked fancy and spanned decades from different companies with her name written on all of them. She was behind her monitor when he stepped forward and crushed the plastic housing with his foot.

'I'm sorry. I didn't see that.' Ethan picked up the pieces.

'Easily done,' Loretta said. 'Just throw it in the bin.'

Throwing it out the window would have been better, but at least it couldn't pump out any more poison. He poured himself a little plastic cup of water from a jug on the table and washed the sickly scent away.

'These photos…' The wall had about ten framed photographs on, all dated with different years.

She looked up from the computer. 'That's an old BBC DJ: David Jenson. You're probably too young to remember him. It was a long time ago.' Another photo showed Loretta at an award ceremony, in a long black dress, with a champagne glass next to an old man.

'That's the director, Woody Allen.'

'Really?' He had heard the name but that's all. She named more people and kept stressing that it was years ago.

'It all feels surreal, like it never really happened.'

'Do you still work with any of them?'

'I can't answer that.'

'Confidential. I get it.' All those letters after her name on her business card, those certificates, and clients made him realise what experience she had. 'I feel special now.'

'Sometimes qualifications scare people off. Those photos bring what I do down to earth.'

'It makes me wonder why you're even bothering with me.'

'I don't help people because they're rich and famous.' She finished up with her email and clasped her hands together as if to say, I'm done. She asked him to sit and get comfortable.

'I liked your old place better,' he said.

'Oh, really?' She took out a packet from a drawer and removed a joss stick. 'Patchouli, OK?' She lit the end and placed it in a stand on the shelf. The end glowed bright, then dulled as smoke rose into the room.

He figured he had about a minute before it reached him.

The window was open an inch. Just enough to let the high street noise creep in. He needed that outside life, not being stuck inside.

A big green rubber plant in the corner of the room sat in a pot of dry earth. It too was planning an escape. It couldn't rely on the Ivy outside the window, moving at a centimetre a day if it was sunny. The rubber plant needed rescuing by a sprinter to prevent its lonely, beige wall, vanilla-scented, Patchouli death. Like a Venus fly trap gang, masked, with guns and tattoos kicking the door in.

Loretta placed her notepad on her lap and was ready to start.

'I'm not feeling it here,' Ethan said. 'Can we go somewhere else?'

Loretta looked puzzled for a moment, then agreed some air would be nice. 'Where would you like to go?'

Ethan had already made his way to the door. 'Somewhere with life,' he said. He looked at the rubber plant on the way out and for a moment he thought the big leaves flapped a little at him. He poured his plastic cup of water into its dirt pot.

'It'll thank you for that one day,' she joked on the way out.

# 4

## SOLITARY FUNK

They settled on the public gardens in the middle of town where dog walkers strolled, and runners lapped with headphones. It had a bench view next to the river with the plaza in the distance. Some skaters were riding the ledges, but he couldn't make out who. At least them being there allowed him to zone out between Loretta's questions. She kept her brown leather gloves on, the ones with a neat seam up the fingers. Her collar was high, and her legs crossed at the knee. She asked how he'd been feeling recently, how the past week had been since they last spoke. He'd been practising his breathing, calm, and slow. She also wanted him to keep a journal, but he couldn't get into that.

'What can you tell me about your mother?'

'I really don't know much.'

'I thought she was in a care home?'

'That's what we tell everyone. People always seemed happier believing we hadn't lost contact, but we didn't want any. '

Loretta said nothing. She did that a lot. It was one of her methods to unwrap private stuff, pick at his truths, and unravel the dumb shit he'd buried.

'And now if we did want to know, we'd have to go back through the system.' Ethan shook his head.

'But do you want to see her?'

'Of course, but it's not going to happen. She's crazy. Our caseworkers said we'd be better off thinking she was dead.'

'They said that?'

'Not exactly. We asked enough times about seeing her, but it never happened. So, fuck it. 'Scuse my French.'

'Can you tell me about a happy time with your family?'

Ethan thought for a moment. Loretta seemed to like it when he went quiet and considered himself. Just as well because piecing memories together was a ball-ache. Many were sketchy like they might not have happened. The first memory he had was of him in the kitchen baking his birthday cake. His mother didn't have enough ingredients and freestyled it with measurements. She figured effort was more important than the results. Making a mess was great fun, and even though he'd be doing all the washing up later whilst she had a needle in her arm, it didn't matter. He felt normal, just like other friend's birthdays he'd heard about. He wondered if they had to wipe the sick off their mother's face too. The fun of baking was shoving all that cake mix in the tray and watching it explode in the oven. The only way to do that, she said, was to sit on the kitchen floor and watch it through the oven door. Big cakes would take nearly an hour and a half. If he didn't sit there. It would burn. And a burnt cake meant a beating. The good thing about cakes though, is it never needed to be perfect. Even the wet mixture was enough to eat with a spoon, it was still cake. Just a wet one.

Later that night his mum would taste his cake with her friends, and he could have all the leftovers he wanted.

Loretta made some notes in a small black notepad. 'Do you have any other fond memories?'

A kid tried to kickflip up onto the big ledge and she nudged him again for an answer.

'I remember this little metal key, hung around mum's waistband. It jangled against her belt loop as she ran up the stairs. I knew the drill and would get inside the cupboard before she could thump me into it. That old smell of cigarette butts is still lodged in my head. The first couple of hours in there were fine, as I could still hear people downstairs, but once the front door had slammed shut, and it went quiet.' Ethan wiped his face.

'Take your time,' she said.

'I'd scream to be let out. It makes me laugh now. I was a stupid little shit then: 'scuse my French. No wonder they shut me in. I'd do the same to me if I were them.'

Loretta wrote more notes and seemed satisfied with his answers. She shut up for a while and was probably bored of listening to people like him complain all the time. A bunch of loons barking on about their lives, moaning at her for a living, must make for a tedious day-job. He imagined her screaming her head off whilst pounding into a punchbag.

'Were you ever able to speak to your mother about any of this?'

He hadn't and couldn't. There was always a sharp pain in his gut and a churning feeling, whenever he thought about it.

The kids across the street began arguing and one snapped the other's board, then they squared up to each other shouting. A third tried to break it up, but the bigger kid just shoved the third out of the way. It was hard to concentrate on Loretta when this was going on.

'Have you tried to get in contact with her?'

'Why would I want to do that?'

None of the kids had punched each other yet, but there was still a chance.

'I believe it could help answer some questions.'

He didn't want any questions answered because he knew what the answers would be. There was no point. 'It's been a long time since you've sat down and spoken with her, maybe she'd be surprised, and pleased to see you?'

'I doubt it.'

'It's been twelve years. You're an adult now and she'll see that too. You might get a completely different reaction. You've grown, you're smarter…' Ethan scoffed at that. '… and time heals. People reflect, feel guilty, and have regrets. They often feel the need to apologise.'

The kids calmed down and went back to skating, and the kid with the snapped board sat and looked through their footage.

Loretta probably figured that her questions had run their course because he didn't have much more to say on the subject. 'What else has been going on? How is work?' she asked.

'It's been OK.' What he really wanted to tell her was his idea. The one Heston put him off. She saw a pained look on his face and pressed him again. 'Can I tell you an idea I've got?' then, 'I've got to skate a handrail this week. 5 days to film, edit and submit, the usual deal, however, the problem is, the rail is as dull as …'

'Excuse your French,' she said.

'Right. Let's just say it's not the most exciting

thing in the world. I need to make it more interesting'

'I don't think I'm going to be able to help you there.'

'Sure, but take it from me, it's boring.' He chewed his lip like his mouth was better off shut. He wasn't supposed to tell anyone outside of N27.

'So, what was the best idea you had?'

She wouldn't blab, he was sure of it. They had their own confidentiality agreement. She never said a word, but it was as if her silence had a way of pulling the words out of him. Damn, she was good.

'I want to blow up the rail as I'm skating it.'

'Excuse me?'

'I want to blow it up. I've got it all planned out. I'm going to pack the underside of the rail with explosives, then box it all in with blocks and hide it beneath a timber frame. We can set up a trigger system so when I get on it, it blows.'

Loretta seemed stunned by his idea and probably wanted to know all the details because her eyebrows lowered and squished together.

'When you say explosives, not real ones?'

Ethan laughed. 'What other kinds of explosives are there? A fake explosion isn't going to look anywhere near as impressive as a real one.'

'And you say you've got it all planned out?'

'I've got a friend who can get me everything: trigger systems, the timer, and explosives. Just a couple of pounds to blow everything across the street. I don't want it looking like a crappy firework.'

She shook her head as if holding back the excitement.

'No-one else knows about it, apart from you, that is. I can't trust anyone. I think someone at work has been sabotaging my missions, so I'm going rogue this time.' He winked at her. 'What do you think?'

'I don't know what to say.'

'I know, right? Insane!'

Loretta stood and put her bag over her shoulder. 'I can't be any part of this. What you've told me is incredibly dangerous, which could cause huge harm to yourself and others. I cannot support you in any way. I urge you to reconsider this and to not follow it through. I can't have anything to do with this.'

'Wait. What? No, hang on. This isn't dangerous. It's all staged. It'll be a stunt for the filming.'

'I know. I heard you. Explosives, flames, blowing debris across the street.' Ethan stood too because she wasn't sitting back down again like people do when they pretend to leave.

'I don't get it. You're leaving? But I'll see you next week, though, right?'

'No. Not at all. I'm terminating our sessions as of now. Our agreement means, I won't contact the authorities, but I may be forced to. My advice is to cease all plans for this idea immediately. You'll have to find someone else to be your therapist.'

The way she spoke sounded final, which didn't make any sense at all. She didn't want Ethan to follow her or ask any more questions. And she had walked away before he could even queue up an apology.

A little blind panic shot through him like he'd lost something valuable. He flipped back to being eight again and felt angry, but there was no-one to be angry at. Calling after her failed, his mouth just fell open where the words should have been. Another loss, like when his mother left him. Now she's doing the same. So much for their deal.

# 5
## SPOT CHECK

The research team's office consisted of three desks: Heston's, James', and a third for an absent member. Heston's chair squeaked as Ethan sat. James had his headphones on, typing until he realised someone was behind him.

'Damn, it's hot in here.' Ethan took off his jacket. 'Are you busy?' He picked up an old Thrasher magazine.

'It never ends,' James said. 'As soon as one project is complete, another deadline is right there staring at me. What are you after?'

'Ideas.' He flicked through the magazine's pages. 'The retail rail is dire. You know about that, right?'

'You made yourself loud and clear about it.'

'What are you working on?'

'Researching the winter season.' James blew

through his cheeks like the thought was painful to hold in. 'We've got our full snow schedule coming up, and it's just one after another. If it isn't snowboarding, it's skiing, if it isn't skiing, it's ice-skating. It's like the winter Olympics up here.'

There was a mountain bike on the far side of the room. 'Is that yours?'

'Yes. It's a bit over the top for commuting, but I can hit the hills on the way home without the risk of destroying it.' James drummed his fingers on his legs. 'So, I've just got to get back to this.' James returned to his emails, or whatever.

Ethan couldn't hide his boredom. The best thing about boredom is all the regular thoughts, like about what to eat, money worries, pain, and family, all get shoved to one side to make room for other thoughts which aren't so easy to figure out.

One such thought struck him that maybe the source of his problems wasn't so far away after all. His old manager Flint had been his headache for some time. She'd never do any dirty work herself and had a million ways to screw with his life, making work more painful than it should have been. He couldn't put his finger on it exactly, but for a moment the Research office just felt convenient, as if it was the source of his problems.

'You've got an empty desk here. Who sits there?'

'Claire,' James said without turning around.

'She's on maternity leave. We've got a temp lined up to come in and work with us.'

When Claire was in the office she was probably fed up, distracted, sweaty, heavily pregnant with the joy of maternity leave and new baby plans. Not exactly the perfect mental state to plan the downfall of a colleague. Then again, he didn't know much about James either. He had been around long enough and recently started delivering Ethan his locations once Ricard's edits started taking off. James was just an office cog, nice enough, but also invisible. No-one paid him any attention.

A balled-up piece of paper bounced off the back of James' head. 'So, my locations each week,' Ethan said. 'I've got some questions.'

'What you want to know?' He grabbed a sheet of A4 from a tray with the schedule on.

'I'm not sure yet.'

On the wall were post-it notes of planning ideas, staff notices, press clippings of stories, and emails. A big yearly calendar pinned to the wall with the Braxton estate marked on it. Nearby were the initials CN.

'Remember when I was at the Braxton estate, and I got knocked out and the camera stolen?'

'A dodgy area.'

'Why was that place chosen? Out of all of them?'

'The granite sculpture.'

'How did you know about it?'

'We had a tipoff from some locals. It's what we do. We ask viewers to send in their ideas.'

'Who was your contact up there?'

'I don't know. Your brother should know.'

'But he's not here, so …'

'What are you getting at?'

The next week on the calendar was the Psychiatric hospital with the initials, VC, next to it.

'What about the Psychiatric Hospital? How did that one come about?'

'Picked from the list you supplied probably.'

'I didn't include that one. Someone else came up with it.'

'I can't remember. Probably another recommendation?'

'That place was even worse. That guy was a complete nutter and I've still got the cuts to show for it. The crazier thing was El Gato. I thought he was going to help me out, but he smashed up my footage and let the guy get away.'

James shrugged as if he was waiting for a question.

'What do these initials mean?' Ethan pointed to the letters CN and then VC. James took off his headphones and came around to the board.

'Oh, those.' James rubbed his chin as if it might summon a genie. 'I'm not sure. They are probably just people we could rely on.'

Ethan had a feeling that James knew exactly what he was looking at. Heston had said that James was meticulous and the analytical one in the team.

'So, CN doesn't mean anything?' Ethan got on James' mountain bike on the other side of the room.

'Hey, be careful with that,' James said. 'It's expensive.'

It was just a bike. There was no reason the get all panicky about sitting on a bike. Ethan repeated his question.

'CN?' James considered. 'Again, your brother might know.'

*Carl Needs* Ethan thought. For some reason, James had Carl's initials on the office board.

Next to the calendar was a map of Ubley and the surrounding areas.

'What do these markings mean?' Ethan pointed them out one-by-one.

James joined him at the wall map. 'These are troubled hotspots. We keep track of any concerns to make sure they don't interrupt filming. This one here,' he pointed at a blue cross, 'indicates a hang-out for drug dealing.'

Ethan pointed at a green cross on the library road. 'And this one?'

'The first sighting of a gypsy camp. We were trying to figure out where they might settle.' James indicated another spot on the map. 'This was another stopping point, and this is where they ended up: at the Leisure Centre.'

'It's not like I could ever forget that one.'

James returned to his seat and took a bite from an apple as people do when they've said too much. His stepdad was always doing that, creating long pauses between accusations. It gave a bit more time to find excuses. James even sat the same way, legs spread, cocky and slumped. It was as if he was saying, *C'mon, what else have you got, boy?*

'I need another filmer for this week.'

James looked surprised initially, then glanced up at the timesheet on the wall. 'Dixel's got a clear schedule. She's available.'

'No, I mean, I *need* someone else. It's not that I have any problem with her work. I just need to freshen up the filming. I want to bring on another filmer just for this week.'

'Is she okay with that?'

'She's fine. I spoke to her earlier. The stats are down, so I want to try something else.'

'I've got Simon.'

'No, I'll sort someone out,' Ethan said. 'It's just that, between you and me, I don't need her to know about it.'

'But you said you spoke to her.'

'I did, but she's not feeling great about it. Best not to mention it. If you could pull some strings and give her something else to do, that's all I'm asking.'

It was clear from James' face that he didn't like the idea of making a late change to the process, but he also saw Ethan's point. N27 needed to get the views back up, so maybe a fresh angle on Ethan's filming would be enough.

'Leave it with me,' James said. 'I'm pretty sure we can come up with something to keep her occupied.'

'Thanks, I appreciate it.' Ethan got up to leave. 'Before I go: do you have the phone number for Hermanez?'

James pulled out his phone and called up his contacts. Sure enough, he had El Gato's number, right there in his favourites.

'You don't want it?'

'No.' Ethan slung his bag on his back. 'I just wanted to know if you had it.'

As soon as he got out of the research office his phone buzzed: Loretta Deane. *Jesus*, he thought, *What do you want now?* He watched the screen vibrate. She probably wanted to apologise, regretting what she said, an error of judgement, bad timing, or something. Whatever it was, Ethan just watched the screen glow until the number cut off. He couldn't stomach her voice right now, and he didn't want to be reminded of how much of an idiot she thought he was. *So much for being professional.* He considered putting a block on her phone number but couldn't spare the thumb energy.

# 6

## HIVES HONEY

After finishing up at N27 Ethan got himself back into town to the retail rail. He needed to check out that spot and get a better look around the local area. Those business units were so new; the ledges and curbs still hadn't had aluminium ground into them. There was even a small loading bay with a mellow bank to a curb. He took one line down from the entrance up the bank for a 5-0 across the top. The thing was as dry as smoked kipper guts. No sooner had he rolled back down the bank than a sixteen-wheeler swung into the loading area almost hitting him. The driver hopped out of a Hives Honey truck in a yellow and black uniform. He had a pen behind his ear, a haircut shaved at the sides, tattoos, and boots good enough for kicking.

'You nearly hit me then,' Ethan said.

'This is a restricted area,' he snapped back.

*All right, keep your hair on,* Ethan thought. A slight smell of marijuana came from the cab. 'Smells like something nice.'

'Mind your own business,' the driver said. The loading bay door opened slowly. Another employee stood in the bay looking at Ethan as if to say, *Who the hell is this?*

The driver got back in the truck, slammed it into gear, and swung it out wide to reverse back onto the bay. Before the lorry had backed up onto the entrance, Ethan saw pallets of shrink-wrapped product waiting to be wheeled in with sack-trucks. There must have been thousands of pounds worth of honey, and another waft of weed coming from the building.

When he jumped out of the truck cab again, he saw Ethan hadn't budged. 'I told you to get out of here.'

He stood so close Ethan could study the pores of the man's skin. 'You need some skin-care on those blackheads.'

The driver tried to grab Ethan's board, but he whipped it away out of reach.

'Uh-uh. No, you don't.'

A side door opened, and an overweight fifties man dressed in an equally oversized beige suit wafted out like a pair of drunk curtains. His grey-black hair was thick enough to find its way out of his ears and nose. A second man appeared. It was Blacker.

*What the hell is he doing here?*

Mr Curtains took a sip from a whiskey glass. 'Everything alright lads?'

'That's one of my staff.' Blacker quickly cut in, as if any delay could have photosynthesised into the wrong shade of opinion. 'Ethan Wares. This is Royston Hives.'

'Ah, the Ubley Ogre!' Royston chirped. 'Good to finally meet the man of the moment.' Ethan glanced at Blacker for some kind of explanation but was met with a fixed smile. 'I'm an appreciator of skateboarding myself,' Hives continued. 'Never did it, obviously.' He tapped his large gut. 'The ballast puts me at a slight disadvantage. My partner's kids used to do it. Anyway, won't you come inside? We've got quite a party planned.'

Royston pushed open the door and they followed the faint sound of music through a corridor. At the end of the hall was an event space the size of a football pitch. It could have held a hundred people inside. The single shop at the front of the building was just the tip of the iceberg. The Hives company had taken over the entire block. Caterers wandered around laying out foods, whilst a band set up on a stage on the far end of the room.

'It's a party for our first three months trading,' Royston announced proudly. 'We're pulling in new contracts all over the Southwest and Midlands worth hundreds of thousands of pounds.'

'Hives Honey is sponsoring N27,' Blacker said. 'Be good to this man, he'll be paying your wages for months to come.'

Royston beamed, 'Well, you know you've got to do your little bit to support businesses, haven't you?'

Blacker patted him on the back. 'And we are very thankful for it too.'

'I hope you like skiffle?' Royston said.

*No-one likes skiffle.*

'And stay for the evening!'

Ethan tried to find the ejector seat button in his pocket. 'I can't. I'm on a deadline. Edits, skating and stuff.'

'Excellent,' Royston said. Ethan could have said anything, and the man would still have heard, *Yes*. 'Fetch yourself a drink. Get comfortable. Have some food.'

As Mr Curtains drifted across the room towards the band, Blacker stretched a grin until it snapped. 'It's lucky you weren't done for trespassing.'

'Technically, you pay me to trespass.'

'But not get caught. Legal have enough to worry about as it is. I can't say I'm impressed. Perhaps, you could find a different place to skateboard?'

'Oh, believe me, I would if I could,' Ethan said. A change of plan would take time, but deadlines in

TV land don't shift. Any delays starting meant more pressure finishing.

Blacker shook his head. 'OK. Just do what you have to do, but remember, he's a sponsor. He's planning to do a lot with us. Sponsoring your new event is one of them.'

'What event?'

'The Ubley Ogre. I must say that when Marketing presented the concept, I wasn't that impressed, but after seeing the materials, I think it's genius. Don't tell me you haven't been given all the details?' Ethan had a blank look on his face. He couldn't find a reply to something he didn't know anything about. 'The Ubley Ogre is you!' Blacker grabbed a handful of Paprika crisps from a bowl. 'You must have seen the life-size cardboard cut-outs dotted around Marketing?'

'Life-size?' Ethan panicked at the thought of him positioned in shop fronts around the city. 'Don't they need my permission to use my image like that?'

'No. Of course not. We own you!' Blacker crunched on the crisps and watched Royston belly-laugh with the band.

'The community support he's giving us is priceless PR,' Blacker stated. 'Don't jeopardise it. Otherwise, I can assure you this will be the last job you will have for a while.' He wandered off towards Royston declaring the excellent choice of music.

. . .

If there was ever a time for an email about the finer details of the Ubley Ogre, or whatever the hell it was, it was now. Yet, no matter how frantically Ethan searched for a good phone signal, he couldn't find a single bar. The building was modern enough and should have been accessible but for some reason there wasn't any Wi-Fi to connect to. Nevertheless, he needed to find out what was going on and tapped out a quick message for a group chat, in the hope that someone would get it and reply.

He was still holding his phone in the air looking for a mobile signal when he reached the food table. The warm chicken wings drizzled in barbecue sauce tasted delicious, and he swallowed several of them before noticing an organisation chart on the wall. It had Royston at the top of the pyramid with employee's underneath. Each one distinctly uglier than the next, including the driver he met outside on the bottom row. It was an org chart from a rejection process, not a selection process. Unless the selection came from HM Prisons.

'Growth!' Royston startled him. 'We've quadrupled in just two months. I can't hire people fast enough. If you ever need a career change, let me know. How about a quick tour? I'll be more than happy to show you around.' Royston had already started moving.

*Why not?* Ethan thought. The skiffle band started to sound like teeth being filed.

The back corridor of the building fed into an open-plan office, which they passed through, left, then right, then through a set of double doors to another set along a corridor. Ethan couldn't help but notice the floor was like glass. Royston pushed through another set of doors into a warehouse. 'And this is where it all happens. A hundred thousand units per day get packed, wrapped, and shipped from here.' The room was a maze of cardboard boxes stacked eight feet high on pallets. A couple of convicts saw them approaching and made themselves scarce.

They passed through many staffing stations and departments for different stages of production until stopping at a much cleaner, clinical environment.

Royston lifted a sterilisation bodysuit off the wall. 'You need to put this on. We can't risk any contamination.' Ethan squeezed into it and slipped a pair of shoe covers on whilst Royston adjusted a hairnet in the mirror.

The cool clean air of the room tasted delicious to breathe as if it had been purified and sprinkled with extra oxygen. Honey samples were laid out on a white work surface.

'Taste this.' Royston handed him a little spoonful of syrup.

Ethan didn't like his food being picked for him,

but at the back of his mind was Blacker's voice saying he shouldn't do anything to ruin their working arrangement. The honey quickly warmed to the temperature of his mouth and melted into a sweet strawberry flavour.

'Great, right? This will be a big seller, I'm sure of it.'

As soon as Ethan was finished with one sample of honey, Royston already had another sample prepared for him to taste, but he declined and changed the subject.

'How did you get into this?' Ethan asked.

'It's been in my family for generations. Bees have always intrigued me. They are one of nature's wonderful creations. Where would we be without them?' Royston left Ethan looking at the labels on the other samples, as he went to the other side of the lab. 'When you think about it. This is just one of mother nature's purest products.' Royston returned and grabbed Ethan's hand.

'Don't move.'

# 7

## THE NIGHTMARE

Royston pulled his hand away and revealed a bee on the back of Ethan's hand. It took a few milliseconds to register those black wire legs crawling across his skin.

'Oh, shit!' He flicked his hand into the air.

The bee took flight in a short, startled loop and landed on the work surface as if nothing had happened. Ethan however, paced around rubbing his wrist in relief.

'Oh, come on now. It's just a tiny bee.' Royston let it crawl back onto his hand and over his fingers.

'No thanks. Keep that thing away from me.'

'They only sting if they're threatened.'

'That's what everyone who's stung by one says. I'm not taking the chance.'

'*He who has overcome his fears will truly be free.* Aristotle said that.'

'Harris who?'

'Aristotle. The philosopher.'

Ethan wasn't sure if that was a question or a statement.

Royston returned the bee to a container and wanted to continue the grand tour. 'Right, that's enough here. Let's move on.' He waved Ethan towards the exit, where they climbed out of their protective suits and pushed through into another corridor. An employee walked in through a fire door on the other side of the room.

'Those damn doors.' Royston pulled hard on the door until it clicked shut.

'They don't shut?'

'We've got the supplier returning to look at the locks, which means the alarms can't be activated.'

Ethan tried to quickly orientate himself to remember that door, however, he couldn't recognise anything through the glass other than some bushes. 'This Ogre event you mentioned earlier. What's that all about?'

'I've got the flyer around here somewhere.' Royston pulled out a leaflet from a drawer and unfolded it. 'They haven't told you about it yet?'

'Oh, sure,' Ethan said. 'But not this version.' The Ubley Ogre was written across the front in a childish font with a picture of him underneath in an animated pose. He recognised it from when there was a wobble board in the office, and someone had taken a picture of him trying it out. The strapline beneath his picture read, *Submit your skateboarding clip to us for a chance to win £1000.* Inside, were shots of kids on skateboards, and a heading, *Find out if the Ubley Ogre can perform your tricks as well as you.* The event was open for any 16 to 24-year-olds willing to take up the challenge. This was a stupid, stupid idea. He noticed he was breathing heavier than usual, and the leaflet lightly quivered in his hand.

'Exciting, isn't it?' Royston beamed. 'We're going to get posters up all around the city and I've personally bumped the money up to £5000 to get some attention.'

'Five grand!' He clamped his mouth and realised every skater would submit footage to win that lump sum. And worse, he knew everyone was going to find it as stupid and as hilarious as he did. With his face all over town, there'd be no hiding. Hives had the money to pimp it on billboards, on the radio, or even a bloody TV advert. Ethan felt his own death staring back at him. He handed Royston back the leaflet and then immediately asked for it back again. 'Can I keep this?'

Royston had no objections. 'Just make sure they send me a new batch once the new versions are done.'

Ethan put the leaflet in his back pocket and tried not to think about it, but he couldn't shake the thought. He checked his phone for a response to his message earlier, but there was still no signal. He needed to get out of it. He had a reputation to protect, the kids would wonder what the hell he was doing, and not to mention everyone else. His old crew would die laughing.

Royston noticed Ethan had fallen behind on the walk. 'C'mon,' he urged. 'There's lots more to see.'

As Royston walked and talked, Ethan knew that the man was just being fed whatever N27 told him. He wasn't the bad guy here; he was ready to sponsor anything they put in front of him. If they offered a Plan B, he'd go with it.

Ethan realised what he needed to do: Get hold of Marketing and ensure they drop the idea. It wasn't too late. He'd come up with some reason why it wouldn't work.

Once they reached the main shop area, Ethan looked across at the polished steel handrail outside. It looked perfect, but just at a terrible angle. The only way to reach it was from the main entrance, but there was no run-up. He then realised there was a warm hum emitting from behind. A huge glass wall held back a brown blur of tens of thousands of bees swarming from floor to ceiling. It felt like his heart crystallised the blood in his veins.

'What the hell is that for?'

'We want to wow people when they walk in.' Royston placed his hand on the glass and felt the buzz. 'We removed the queen to keep them agitated.'

Set within the wall was an ordinary brown door with a swipe card door lock.

'What's back there?'

'That's the entrance to your worst nightmare.' Royston winked and smiled. 'More bees!' he laughed, then, 'I've got to head back to the party. You'll be fine to let yourself out, won't you?' Royston pointed at the front doors and reminded Ethan to give them an extra push to lock after leaving.

Once he was on his own, Ethan placed his hand on the glass wall and instantly felt the vibration of insects humming as they danced. He put his ear up to the glass and felt his jaw rattle his teeth.

'Vicious little bastards.'

The door in the wall suddenly unlocked and an employee stepped out. He wasn't wearing a bee suit, and there wasn't a swarm billowing out behind him. It was just another room and one which wasn't on the guided tour.

As the employee headed back out into the warehouse, Ethan noticed a key card pass on the counter. Royston must have removed it from the drawer whilst looking for the leaflet. He tried it on one of the doors and the LED on the lock flicked from red to green. He pushed through into another long corridor. He looked through a small porthole window and went into another room which was split in two; one side was a workshop and the other was full of desks. Judging by the posters on the walls and sketches on the whiteboards, it was a type of design or development space. More importantly, there were things to skate. The aisle had square concrete flowerpots, metal benches, small steps, and well-built filing cabinets. He looked back out again towards the shopfront builder's area and noticed the pallets and sheets of plywood. There were different types of plastics and containers and barrels.

This place had a good feeling about it and an idea started to form, but first, he needed a filmer, and he knew exactly where to start looking.

# 8

## HAPPY SHOPLIFTER

Outside the Happy Shopper on the Eastfield council estate, two grubby men in their mid-twenties passed a bottle between them. CCTV already had them under surveillance. The CCTV in question was an ISPOOP hired security guard, Malcolm, who hadn't even looked up from his phone.

Ethan skated up the path, jumped off his board, and tried to spot his old mate Chris through the windows. With no sign of him behind the tills, Ethan knew where to look. Whenever it wasn't busy or with no chance of the manager turning up, Chris would sneak out the back of the shop for a skate in his extended lunch breaks.

'I thought I might find you here.'

Chris saw Ethan approach. 'What do you

want?' He picked his phone up and switched off the recording.

*At least, he's talking to me.* 'Before you start, I just want to say, sorry.'

Chris huffed. 'I shouldn't even be talking to you after what you did to us.'

'I know I've been an idiot, but you guys have got to start speaking to me some time. What have I got to do to apologise?'

'Maybe there's nothing you can do? You're still skating and being paid.'

'For N27? That's the only company who'd take me.'

'Whilst I'm in a newsagent or haven't you noticed?' then, 'What do you want?'

'I need a filmer for a work project. It's well paid, quick, and you're the man I need for it.'

'You're working for a media company, and they don't have access to any cameramen? I cry bullshit.'

'Okay, well, the one I've got isn't cutting it. Her edits are nowhere near as good as yours.'

'Whatever you're offering it better be good.'

'Money?'

'Is that all? Thanks, but no thanks.' Chris turned his camera back on and went back to flipping and filming.

Ethan sat and watched him skate.

All he could offer was money which should have been enough to start repairing a friendship. He couldn't fathom how hurt someone had to be after a year apart and still be that annoyed at him. He and Chris had toured together, spending months on the road, and lived the pro-life until it all went bad. Now, just being in the same postcode stank and couldn't be washed clean with an acid bath. What good would an apology be when he could offer the cold hard cash of work to buy stuff for a month? It just didn't sit.

Ethan remembered Heston saying that N27 would never allow the Hives retail rail to be blown up. And sadly, he was right. It was reckless, dangerous, and stupid, but it was still the most exciting thing he could think of. Chris needed a hook, too. Only another skater would recognise that a regular edit wouldn't be good enough. If N27 was trying to make his life difficult, then why not put a rocket up its ass and shoot it into space?

Ethan had an idea.

'This week, we're going to do something no-one has ever done before.' Chris merely looked over which was all Ethan needed. 'I'm going to set the Hives rail on fire and blow it up like in Fully Flared.'

'Are you kidding?'

'Nope.' He let the words sink in, trying not to sound desperate. His damn mouth was always getting him into trouble, and now here he goes again. Up until now, he hadn't told anyone apart from Heston, and Loretta didn't count as they had *confidentiality*.

'Fully Flared wasn't a random job,' Chris said. 'It was a film set, with crews, experts, and health and safety teams. Is the network paying for all that?'

'Not exactly. I'm doing it myself with their budget.' Chris was already huffing at the ridiculousness of it. 'This is better because we're in control. If we leave it to them, they'll screw it up, or make it so crappy people will only watch it to see how stupid we look.'

'We? Don't you mean, you?'

Ethan was getting fed up with everyone he told focusing on the wrong details. He was certain, more than ever, that this was the best idea he ever had.

'Don't worry. I'll figure everything out. I've got contacts that can get me all the materials. It might sound risky, but what have you got to lose?'

'Oh, just my Uni application, my job, and my future because of a criminal record.'

'You're not going to get a criminal record. Don't be ridiculous. And I wouldn't be asking you if I didn't need your help. Thousands of people are going to see this, and your name will be on the edit. We can do this. Are you in?'

An almighty crash came from inside the shop. It was the sound of shelving and products clattering onto the floor. Chris looked through the door and just saw a tangle of legs kicking around.

# 9
## AUDI TT

Malcolm was wrestling with one of the smack addicts, throwing punches in a one-on-one battle which was fun to watch. The second smack-head, however, was upfront, hunched over the shop counter, snatching and pocketing anything of value. Occasionally Malcolm got the upper hand and it looked like he didn't need any help, but then some punches would land.

'You want to give him a hand?' Chris asked Ethan. 'You're bigger than me.'

'I think your man has got it under control.'

Reluctantly, Chris grabbed the man by the back of the collar and tried to yank him off Malcolm. Ethan figured two-on-one was enough and went to deal with the second man helping himself to cigarettes and razor blades. Ethan acted like a customer and let him finish, but then as the man dove over the counter, he went back for the charity box. Whilst his back was turned, Ethan flipped his board over, and swung it like a baseball bat into the side of the man's head. Gravity did the rest. It took a good few seconds before he started moving and the low-groan of head-hugging pain came out of his mouth. Meanwhile, at the back of the shop, the smack-head had wriggled out of Malcolm's grip, got to his feet, and sprinted towards the exit. Ethan tripped his feet, which sent him crashing into the door, and out into the street.

*Sod him. One's enough,* Ethan thought.

Chris made a half-hearted attempt to chase after him but gave up easily. He wasn't getting a hepatitis spit-ball in his eye for minimum wage.

Malcolm wandered to the front of the shop rubbing out the pain in his shoulder. 'Where were you whilst they were destroying the place?'

'Your job title is literally, Security! You're supposed to be the muscle, not me.'

'Hello?' Ethan interrupted. 'Who cares? We've got one shit-bag.'

Malcolm picked up the dazed and disorientated thief and tried to question him, but it was pointless.

A bright white Audi TT swung into the parking bay outside. It was the boss, Tony Bentini.

'Oh, great,' Chris said. 'What were the chances of him turning up?'

'One-hundred percent,' Malcolm said. 'I hit the silent alarm.'

The irate Italian burst through the door all late and pointless. 'What the hell has happened? I leave you people here to look after the place. You're supposed to do your job and what is this? My shop is destroyed.' Tony saw two people on the floor: the smack-head flat out on his stomach and Ethan against the counter. 'At least you've caught these two.'

'It's nothing to do with me,' Ethan said. 'Talk to your staff.'

'He's not one of them,' Chris said.

'He looks like trouble. What are you doing here?'

'Wasting my time, clearly.'

'Don't worry. He's with me,' Chris said.

Whilst Tony surveyed the damage, Malcolm told how the men ransacked the place. All the details were painted favourably towards his own actions, and he barely managed to mention any contributions by Chris and Ethan. Tony wound an invisible wheel with his finger in the air, encouraging Malcolm to get on with it until he had heard enough.

'Chris. Tidy this up and get the shop back in order.' Tony guided Malcolm to the back of the shop for a private word. When Tony returned, he had a different tone. 'You were outside again?'

Chris knew exactly what Malcolm had done. 'I was trying to rescue your muscle from being pummelled by a skinny rat. If it wasn't for us, your useless security wouldn't have caught anyone.'

'How many times have I told you about skateboarding? I'm not paying you to be out there. This is exactly why I employ people. At least Malcolm was doing his job.'

'He'd been glued to his phone all morning.'

'I don't think you're taking this job seriously,' Tony snapped back. 'I don't need people like you here. Get your stuff and get out. You're fired.'

'This is not cool. You can't do that.' Chris' defence was futile. He was expendable and knew it. Tony could just hire another local kid tomorrow and everything would be back to normal for him.

'Get out of here,' Tony insisted. 'And take your friend with you.'

Chris didn't protest any more, he just went to the backroom, grabbed his bag and board, and slammed the door as he left.

'Can you believe that guy? I gave them three months of hard labour and for what? Nothing.'

It was weird seeing Chris stress out about a job that he hated. However, Ethan just wanted to say, *Screw that guy, join me.*

'That's my summer blown now,' Chris said. 'So much for banking some cash before Uni.'

'Look, I know you said *No* back there,' Ethan

said. 'But my offer is still on the table. £180 a day. It's only a week's work, but better than nothing.'

'I dunno, man.' Chris shook his head and walked on contemplating his options. There was not a lot going for it. Jobs were hard to come by and the summer was flying by so quickly, they'd soon be into the winter.

'Dammit. If anybody else finds out about this, they're going to ostracise me too.'

'They can't ostracise you. You haven't done anything. I'm the one they've got the problem with, not you.' At that moment Ethan's phone buzzed in his pocket. It was Loretta again. 'Jesus, why won't this woman leave me alone.'

'Is that your girlfriend or something?'

'No. Someone's been bugging me for the past couple of days.'

'So, answer it?'

'She can sweat a little bit.' Ethan put his phone away. 'So, will you help me?'

Chris shook his head like he was flipping a risky coin around. 'Okay,' he said eventually. 'I'll do it.'

'Yes, mate.' An immediate sense of relief hit Ethan at a problem solved. They bumped fists. 'Glad to have you on-board.'

The same feeling didn't appear on Chris' face. He looked like he'd just lost a fat lump of cash in a card game. The man needed cheering up.

'Are you ready to go bomb shopping?'

## 10

## PYROTECHNICS

Ethan and Chris met the next morning and took the bus through the south of the city. The trip reminded him of a journey to London on the bus with a fat man snoring between them. They threw Haribo over the man's head into Chris' mouth, until Ethan hit him on the side of the face. He woke with a grumpy snort as if someone had fired a water pistol at him. Chris was staring out of the window trying to stifle a laugh as the man hollered around the seats, *Who did that?* They then made a pact to do it again whenever they travelled.

'So, we are going to a film studio?' Chris asked. 'How the hell did you arrange that?'

'It's not a film studio. The company sells and supplies sets and equipment to the film industry. They might get a few calls a year, but those orders can be worth hundreds of thousands of pounds each. My mate's dad has arranged for us to do a bit of shopping.' Ethan pulled a packet of Haribo out of his pocket and shook it with a mischievous smile.

'Sweet. So, why are we going?'

'To collect the gear. We've only got one chance to get this right.' Ethan put the sweets back in his pocket. He pressed himself back into the seat, put his head against the glass, and let the buildings zip past.

Once the bus arrived at its stop and dropped them off, they coughed their way through the diesel fumes and turned right down Shipham Lane. They passed the recycling shop, the garage, and some other empty units heading towards a shabby grey warehouse. The building had no sign, door number, or letterbox.

'It doesn't even look open,' Chris said.

'It doesn't have to.' Ethan knocked and waited. 'It's invite-only.' He knew the owner would be looking through the spyhole in the door at them. He hated that. Then the door opened to a fat man in an old navy-blue wool jumper, he looked bothered and picked food out of his teeth with a dirty fingernail.

'We're here to pick an order,' Ethan said. 'Name: Bryon Dunkley.'

When the name registered, he nodded and invited the lads inside.

The place smelt of cold timber and cement dust

and contained huge racks of metal shelving, three floors high. The man introduced himself as Harris and walked around to his desk to find the order.

'Here you go.' He handed the paperwork to Ethan. 'Grab a trolley. All the bin codes are on the sheet and all the product codes are at the end of the shelving racks. Anything you can't find, give me a shout.'

'It looks dead here,' Chris said. 'What do you do all day?'

The man pointed towards the TV in the office. 'I watch Disney films.'

Chris laughed and then realised the man's smile was as straight as the flat-earth YouTube videos he probably watched. 'Oh, you're serious? Ok, that's cool.'

Ethan looked over the list and walked towards the wood section, whilst Chris went to get some wheels. They needed two, eight by four, eighteen-millimetre balsa wood sheets and loaded them onto the trolley.

'These are as light as paper,' Chris said.

'And they damage like paper too.'

Next on the list: packing blocks. They went round to the next shelving rack and lifted a dozen into the cart.

'These are a joke too.' Chris held a pack of four up with one hand and loaded them in.

The next thing on the list was trigger cable.

Ethan found the cable aisle and skim-read all the labels until he found the right one. 'We need three metres.' He stretched lengths out along a measuring stick, then added another couple of metres, and cut it. Next: batteries. There wouldn't be any power source available so a few packs of AA batteries would do it. The next section: Incendiaries.

They found shelves of small paper packages printed with codes. 'This is the dangerous stuff,' Ethan said pointing to the warning signs on the racking. He ran his finger across the labels looking for the correct weight.

Chris read a safety leaflet. 'This stuff is really dangerous.'

'Relax. Not until a charge is wired through it. Apparently, it's just like Plasticine.'

'Apparently? Apparently, isn't convincing me you know what you're doing.'

'I'll get two packs, just to be sure. I can't afford for this to be a damp squib.'

'You're kidding?' Chris said, but Ethan had already moved on to the next aisle.

It wasn't just a matter of shopping to set the blast up. Ethan needed a worrying invoice to land on the desk of Finance, so someone at N27 would panic and contact management. It was the only way he could guarantee someone would try to stop him. Chris didn't need to know this though. He was already asking too many questions and inevitably try and talk him out of it like Heston and Loretta. He didn't want to risk stressing another friendship.

Next on the list was a triggering mechanism, found in a completely different, cleaner section of the warehouse. All the little devices were neatly laid out on shelves and illuminated by bright white lamps from above. Everything seemed to sparkle and shine.

'This is the most expensive part of the purchase.' Ethan scanned the shelves for the correct system. 'FX3G Series Logic Module. This is it. £899.' The small clear plastic case held a circuit board packed with wires, LEDs, and cable connectors. All the other materials in the cart felt like he was building a garden shed, but this was like something out of Hurt Locker. 'I'm glad Bryon is wiring this, not me. I wouldn't know where to start.'

That was the last of the main items. The rest of the list had only generic stuff like nails, a hammer, gaffer tape, and two tins of grey paint to cover the wooden panels. With the order done, they took the cart back to reception where Harris went over the contents. Ethan confirmed N27s invoicing details and delivery address, then signed the order form.

'I'll get this packaged up and dropped off by tomorrow morning,' Harris said.

'We need it sooner than that. Would you do a rush job and get it there by the end of today?'

The man seemed a bit troubled by this.

'Jesus. It's not like you've got anything else to do here.'

Harris clenched his thinking teeth, then tilted his head like he was cornering hard.

Ethan hadn't finished. He knew when to lay into a slacker. 'You're just going to sit on your fat ass eating cakes and watching Frozen. Come on, pull your finger out, Little Princess.'

A single second of quiet passed so slowly, Chris felt he had to say something: to laugh, or duck, or something. Suddenly Harris broke into a spittle-spraying belly-laugh. It took the man a couple of seconds to get his composure back and wipe the tears from his eyes.

'OK. Leave it with me,' he chuckled whilst walking back to his office, 'but don't go making a habit of it!' he shouted.

## 11

## N27 COLLECTION

From the window of the burger bar, they watched the entrance of N27. It was near the end of the day and between them, they'd seen all the employees leave: Heston, Bennett from accounts, and Blacker too.

'You're not eating?' Ethan bit into a double.

'Do you know much sodium is in those things?' Chris flipped over a menu list in search of the nutritional contents.

The poster on the wall next to them had a huge photo of a burger with the saturation levels pumped up to eleven.

Ethan tapped it with his finger. 'Look at the colours in that bun.'

'Exactly: colours. Artificial ones.'

'It's got everything I need: the five basic food groups.'

'You can't even name three of the five basic food groups.'

Ethan thought for a moment. 'Meat. Bread. Fries.'

'I think I'll stick with my water.'

'Since when did you become such a food expert, anyway?' Ethan bit into his burger. 'You used to eat these all the time. You were worse than me.'

'I found out what was in them.'

'Those were the best days. Chip fights in the van as we belted down the M5. What I'd give to go back to that.'

'You should have thought of that before you…'

'Here's our man.'

A white transit van pulled up outside N27. Harris got out, went around to the back doors, and heaved out a pallet onto the floor. Any spectator would have seen superhuman strength, but those blocks were basically Styrofoam. He put everything on a trolley and wheeled it round to reception. Dennis took one look through the doors and waved the man around to the side. They chatted briefly, whilst Harris signed the paperwork, then pushed the trolley through the building. It was another few minutes before the man returned to his van and left.

Ethan put the last piece of burger in his mouth and took another sip of coke. 'Are you done?'

'Done? Did I even start?'

. . .

The two friends stepped through N27s entrance like it was normal to be there after hours. It wasn't, but Dennis wasn't particularly sharp on staff routines what with still being in his three-month probationary period.

'Working late?' Dennis asked.

'Something like that,' Ethan said.

Chris signed the guestbook and then went out to the goods-in bay.

Ethan slapped the pallet a few times like a prized bull at a showground. 'I told N27s legal team they'll need to increase their insurance this week, like up to £1 million.'

Bryon's camper van pulled into the loading area. He jumped out and fed his arms into a bland navy jacket. 'Is that everything?' he asked?

Ethan handed him the order list. 'It looks good.'

Bryon looked over the list and the began loading everything into the van. There was no rush, they had another hour of daylight to kill before starting the dangerous work of packing out the retail rail.

## 12

## PREPPING THE RAIL

It took several trips around the centre until Bryon found a parking space. He then climbed into the back, squeezed past the pallet, and looked out through his curtains. It was still too busy and too light outside.

'We need to wait for everyone to head off,' he said. 'Probably another hour from now before we can get started.' He measured one of the blocks against his hand. 'We only need them half that size.' He took a hammer and chisel out from under his bench seat and handed them to Ethan.

'Why me?'

'You bought them,' Bryon said. 'Besides, you'd only blame *us* if things went wrong.'

Chris laughed. 'I don't know about you guys, but I'm buzzing already.' He bounced his knee up and down like he had German Techno in his head. 'Anyone else?'

'No. It looks like you've got enough adrenaline for all of us.' Ethan peered through the curtains at the rail and thought about security. 'How are we going to do this?'

'I thought you were the one with the plan?' Chris said.

'I got us this far, or haven't you noticed?'

'Nothing's happening until dark,' Bryon said. 'So, settle back. We've got some time to kill.'

Everything in the van needed unpacking. The more preparation they did now, the faster the whole build would be. Bryon sliced away the shrink-wrap with a knife, wound it into a ball and threw it over the back seats. Next, he separated all the items as best he could in the remaining space. Before Chris had untangled his headphones and found a playlist, Bryon had pulled out his toolbox, started stripping away cable ends and crimping connectors together on the triggering system. When he finished, the device looked like something the Predator would give birth to.

Ethan slid the door open, startling Chris, and let the cold air into the van. 'I think we're good to go. A guard let the last employee out and locked the front door.'

The atmosphere of the streets had changed from traffic jammed commuters heading home on foot, bike, and car, to the hum of taxis dropping off evening diners, and the flappity-clatter of buses spewing evening revellers onto the streets.

Bryon passed out some blocks to Ethan. One swift tap in the centre with the chisel split them apart like a piece of frozen bread.

'How many of these do I need to do?'

'All of them.' Bryon inspected the stack of balsa wood sheets, whilst Chris went to measure the rail dimensions, angle, step height, and depth. With them, Bryon was able to mark out the exact cut points.

'You've bought too much charge,' Bryon realised. 'This will blow the whole rail to pieces.'

Ethan snorted block dust out of his nose. 'I figured you'd play it safe.' He whacked the chisel into another block. 'I don't need a Health & Safety lecture, and I also don't need a reminder of the worst-case scenario. This is all my risk. You won't be anywhere near it.'

'What about me?' Chris stressed.

'When we shoot the rail, pan out wide and you'll be clear of it. Trust me.'

'Trust you?' Bryon said. 'I'm beginning to think you've got a screw loose. You do realise if this thing triggers by accident you'll be blown across the road?'

'You're kidding. Look at this stuff.' Ethan broke a block in half over his head. 'It's like we've raided a joke shop. Are you sure there isn't some silly string left in the van? Everything's going to be fine.'

'It's your funeral.' Bryon said.

With all the cut blocks packed into the van again, Bryon u-turned across the road and parked it right up alongside the rail. He heaved out an old electrician's tent and put it up around the rail. Before the sides were buttoned-down, Ethan and Chris began moving all the materials inside. Bryon then drove the van to the other side of the street before joining the others back inside the tent. They worked quickly and quietly stacking the blocks and taping them to the underside of the rail. Between each row, Bryon laid slithers of charge into the gaps, so Ethan could tape them in place. As each row connected to the next, Bryon kept letting out a sigh of relief like he expected it to blow up at any moment. The final row required some delicate block cutting to make everything fit until he was happy.

Ethan picked up the leftover charge and considered the rail.

'Don't even think about it.' Bryon looked at him like he was a maniac. 'I've used as much as I can.'

It was at that moment the shadow of a security guard silhouetted against the tent.

## 13

## EN GUARD!

Bryon signalled everyone to be quiet and pointed at the moving figure. He put on a fluorescent waistcoat, grabbed a hardhat off the floor, and stepped outside. Chris and Ethan kept quiet and low at the back, uncertain what would happen next.

'Have you got permission to be here?' It was almost certainly a guard from Hives Honey.

'We're just doing some maintenance on a troublesome rail,' Bryon said. 'It's worked loose from its fitting and needs boarding up.'

'Kind of late to be doing this,' the guard said.

'The boss said we should do it when pedestrians wouldn't get in the way.'

The conversation went quiet for a moment, whilst the guard considered his next move. 'And which company do you work for? Have you got some paperwork?'

'Of course. Just a minute.'

Chris looked petrified and Ethan shook his head as if to say *Don't worry*. Within a few seconds, Bryon must have handed the man some credentials.

'Here you go. Hendricks Maintenance Services. The number's on there. Call the boss of you like, but if I were you, I wouldn't bother. He's not going to be up yet, and he'll be grumpy as hell if you call him.'

'Forged papers,' Ethan whispered to Chris. Bryon was good like that; he could plan his way out of anything.

'Okay,' the guard said after a moment. 'Everything measures up here.'

Paperwork exchanged hands. The shadows outside shifted from left to right and back again, then split in two as the guard moved towards the building. Until he stopped.

'Mind if I look?' A hand grabbed the tent door.

'We're all done now,' Bryon said. 'I'm just packing up.'

'We?' the guard said. 'Who's we? I thought you said it was just you?' The guard's hand-pulled open the doorway, just as Ethan slid out the rear of the tent. Torches swung around and Bryon must have been relieved to find no-one inside. Outside, the friends froze like boulders, low and close on the floor with just a millimetre of fabric between them and the guard.

'See. I told you was just me. I said *We* but I meant *the company*.'

'Right,' the guard said. 'And this is just a temporary fix?'

'Sure. It'll be completely repaired in a couple of days.'

The guard seemed satisfied, and the voices moved back outside the tent. Ethan and Chris moved quietly around the opposite side to stay out of sight. When the guard finally moved back towards the building, they sprinted across the street and into Bryon's van.

'That was too close.' Chris gently closed the door.

Ethan checked through a gap in the side curtains in case the guard had seen them running.

A minute later Bryon joined them back in the van. 'I thought we were done for then.' He took off his hardhat and wiped his forehead.

They waited to make sure the guard didn't return, but after a few minutes, they knew they had to get back to the rail and finish up. The hard work was done, but the wiring still needed to be completed. They agreed that Bryon should do this alone in case the guard came back.

It took another fifteen-minutes before Bryon appeared out of the tent with the used tins of paint. He packed up all the tools and brought everything back to the van. Chris and Ethan shuffled things around to make space as Bryon returned to the tent, collapsed it, and carried it back under his arm.

'Everything is set,' he said with relief. 'You'll have to pour lighter fluid across the top when you're ready to film it. Once your truck flips the switch, a spark will set the whole rail on fire. Then when you get to the end another switch will connect with your back truck and trigger the explosion. There'll be a one-second delay. So, manual off the end. If your front truck hits the trigger, it'll go off too early.'

'And take my eyebrows off, right?' Ethan joked.

'Not just your eyebrows, you idiot. Your legs, too.' Ethan laughed nervously, but Bryon continued, 'The one-second delay should give you enough time to start rolling away. But,' he stressed, '*only* if you manual *over* the switch.'

'Yeah, yeah. Whatever.'

'So, what now?' Chris asked.

'That's it. I'm done. The rest is up to you guys tomorrow. You want me to drop you off?'

Chris nodded, 'Thanks.'

'I'm not going back yet,' Ethan said. 'I might skate around the plaza for a bit. You guys go ahead. And Chris, thanks for the help. I'll see you all tomorrow.' Ethan fist-bumped the pair and watched Bryon pull away from the curb.

. . .

The Hives Honey building looked spooky in the dark, as the amber light of the front windows seemed to ghost out over the steps and cast an eerie jagged shadow. They'd made a great job of the rail work. Even that lick of dull grey paint blended everything boringly into the background. It would be dry within a couple of hours, and by the morning people will be walking up and down them without even realising what was under all that framework.

The mild evening's breeze picked up around the tree cover and someone walked out of the shadows into the streetlight heading straight for the rail.

It was a figure he recognised instantly.

There was only one person he knew with crutches.

## 14

## KUNG FOOL

Heston's right toe scuffed the ground in the way that it does as each crutch clicked up the path. He stopped at the rail and looked at the trigger mechanism. With one crutch leant against his arm, he dabbed the wet paint and examined the fit between the rail and the wood.

Ethan wondered why his brother didn't phone ahead. It wasn't like him to turn up unannounced as he usually preferred to grab a lift. It dawned on him that he'd been waiting for someone, not today, necessarily, and not this person specifically. He knew someone would interfere in his attempts to film, someone would intervene in the process which would cause chaos for his week, and yet, there, in front of him, was his brother digging into the electronics of his big idea.

He curiously watched from afar, then felt bewildered as he tried to match up this new information with his assumptions. Eventually, he realised how damned annoyed he'd gotten.

'Hey, bro. What are you doing?'

Heston's expression turned to shock when he realised who it was approaching him from across the street. 'Jesus, you startled me. What are you still doing here? I thought you'd left.' Heston steadied himself back on both crutches.

'Why didn't you come over and say hello when we were setting up?'

His words seemed to bubble and spit with the surprise of the moment. 'I was just in the area, and I thought I'd… It looked like you guys over there, but I was just leaving you to it.' Heston looked up and down the street, then squinted, and shrugged. 'What? I can't go out at night without your permission?'

'It's you, isn't it? You've been setting me up each time.'

'What are you talking about?' Heston stuttered thoughts like dumb bullets.

'Why?' No matter how closely Ethan listened for an essence of truth, all he could hear was his brother scratching around for an answer. Heston usually had one, but for some reason, that evening, whatever Heston did, it stank of wrongs. Week old ones left out of the fridge for days and crawling with maggots.

'That's ridiculous!' He blurted into the night air. It was the first line of defence and a universal declaration to the Gods of *What-the-fuck?* 'Where do you get your stupid ideas? I said I was in the area. What do you mean, *It's me?*'

His bravado felt like a bubble which could be popped with a touch. Weirdly flimsy. He hadn't seen his brother so lost for smart words before. It didn't matter that he was on crutches or eighteen-months older. It didn't matter how good a skater he used to be, or that they were on the same team, and shared so many good times.

The cause of all his problems at N27 was staring him in the face.

'So, the smarter older brother isn't that smart after all.' Ethan felt like a headache was coming on. A strange relief and a huge rage conflicted in his head. He wanted to sit and think, but his legs wouldn't let him. Loretta taught him to take deep breaths at times like this when his mind felt stuffed, but those breaths weren't working right now.

Contempt crept in.

It *was* his brother. It all made sense. 'All those locations I've been going to. All those screw-ups.'

Heston searched for answers to deflect his brother and claim his innocence, but Ethan was on a roll.

'You've always been pissed at me being able to skate after the crash, and you were the one who suggested I pay for your recovery. You've been taking over half my wages.' Ethan noticed he was pacing and remembered sitting in the office with James, and that calendar over Heston's desk marked with dates and initials, El Gato's phone number, the map of the gypsy sites. His certainty solidified. 'I remember overhearing a call at work and I now know you were speaking to El Gato. I've seen the call history on your phone. I've seen emails on your computer and didn't put it together before.'

'So what?' Heston bit back. 'Do you have any idea how hard it is to look after you and your stupidity?' This is what Ethan wanted: an explanation. 'You're an imbecile without me. You'd be screwed.' Heston stepped forward and pushed Ethan back. Almost immediately, Ethan lashed out and hit his brother in the face. Heston knew the hit was coming and let the first punch happen. It was the trigger he needed to retaliate. The brothers lunged at each other and fell quickly to the floor in a tangle of grappling and flailing fists with powerless punches.

Some men across the road saw a thug lash out at a person on crutches and ran over with his friends. Ethan was yanked back by his collar but lashed out with his elbow and connected with the bridge of the man's nose. Ethan jumped back onto

Heston and another man tried to pull him away. Eventually, they both realised they were being held back from thumping the facts out of each other and turned on the samaritans.

'What the hell are you doing?'

'Leave us alone!'

'Can't brothers have a fight in peace?'

The three men looked confused, then let the brothers go as the realisation sank in. 'Who the hell fights their brother who's on crutches?' the first man said.

'Idiots,' the second man said, then pulled his friends away to carry on with their evening.

Once Ethan realised the men weren't coming back, the fight caught up with him. Their energy had been spent and the motivation to continue had passed. They both sat on the curb.

'I haven't had a good scrap like that for ages.' Ethan sucked on his numb lip. 'Have I got any red on me?'

Heston looked briefly then went back to feeling his ribs. 'You landed a couple of good ones too.'

'More than a couple.' Ethan still didn't have the answers he needed. 'Ever since I joined the company, you've been working to screw things up for me?'

'Of course not. But you weren't going to change.'

'What does that mean?'

'I knew you'd ruin things for yourself. You're a walking catastrophe. If I hadn't stepped in, you'd have lost your job. I'm able to use up your health benefits as long as you're employed, remember? *I'd* have lost it all and *you'd* have nothing. I've been looking out for you. Protecting you from yourself. All your daft decisions I've had to deal with. Your *Slings and Arrows*.'

Ethan let his brother shout it all out, but he didn't hear a thing of value. He just thought about them growing up in the care system, switching homes, keeping secrets from caseworkers, and promising to keep each other safe in future. Their pact. And now it felt like he had knives in his back. And Heston made it sound like those knives were needed, and the pain he felt was needed.

'But why couldn't you just tell me?'

'Because you blab everything to everyone! You can't even hold a white lie.'

'We've been lied to enough over the years! I can't do it anymore.'

'So, you'd rather suffer than save yourself? If you're telling everybody everything, then you're giving everything away about yourself. You need to hold some stuff back.'

'Who else knows about this? Ricard? James? Flint?'

'They all know. Everyone knows you're your own worst enemy.'

'Even Dixel?' Ethan didn't need an answer, it was written all over Heston's face. 'You're my brother. You're supposed to be looking out for me.'

'What do you think I've been doing?'

Ethan's eyes itched. He blinked away the discomfort for a few seconds until quiet tears appeared. Heston couldn't see how red and puffy his eyes became, but the streetlights lit a wet streak down his cheek that glistened under his chin. He finally uttered, 'Flint never wanted me in this job anyway. She wanted Ricard all along. She wanted me out. You wanted me out. If they want it so badly then I'll walk. I can't do this anymore. I'm done. I quit.'

## 15

**LOST AND FOUND**

'Don't be stupid. You can't quit. This is exactly what I've been trying to prevent. You're under contract. If you walk away from this job, or even if you're fired, you'll get nothing. No cash, no benefits.'

'You think I care about the money? And you can't believe for one minute that I give a shit about N27. I'd rather be on my own and do my own thing.'

'You don't know the half of it.' Heston explained how Ethan's contract had an anti-competition clause, which prevented him from doing any similar job for a year after leaving. 'You can't skate for money. Any money. You'll be sued. The only way out of this is to be released from your contract. They have to let you go. It has to be their decision, not yours.'

'I can't film or put my edits online?' Heston shook his head. 'I can't skate for another company?' Again, Heston shook his head. 'I can't do anything. Can I?'

'You can't earn any money from your skateboarding. You *can* work in a supermarket for the next year or do some other dead-end job, but *nothing* in the industry or you'll be sued.'

'I'm not going to sit back and let it happen,' Ethan said.

'If you go ahead and do this rail stunt the consequences could be huge.'

'So, I'm screwed no matter what?'

Heston didn't need to reply, Ethan knew the answer.

'Either way, I'm not losing my job over this,' Heston said. 'I can't even back you up if it goes wrong. You're on your own.'

A buzz came from Ethan's pocket. It was Loretta Deane again. 'What is it with this woman?'

'It's a bit out of hours to call you, isn't it?'

He let the phone buzz away. 'She's trying to talk me out of doing this rail thing.'

'Good. Listen to her.'

Ethan sighed and put the phone to his ear. 'If you're calling again to tell me what I shouldn't be doing. Don't bother. I got the message last time.'

'No, wait. I'm sorry.'

He mouthed to his brother, 'She's now apologising.'

'I'm sorry for what I said. I was worried and over-reacted. I'm not here to tell you what you can or can't do. I can't stop you, but after our conversation, I found out some information about your mother.'

She instantly got his attention. Just the mention of his mother froze his thoughts and he sat forward with a wrench in his gut. Heston realised something serious was up.

'Your mother was released from care four years ago and has been confirmed as living at the Ubley Estate.'

Loretta sounded professional like she usually does, but he couldn't comprehend what she was saying. If his mother was living so close, then they'd know about it.

'Mum's living in Ubley?' Ethan looked at Heston. Loretta stressed that he had heard her correctly. 'Are you sure you've got the right person?'

'Yes. It's the same Catherine Wares. She's not being held for any medical or psychiatric reasons. Sorry, I don't have much time now, but I'll send you all the details and please don't tell anyone where this information came from. It could risk my professional integrity and our client, patient relationship. But more importantly, the reason why I'm telling you is I believe you should go and speak to her. It'll either provide you with some answers or give you some closure for your relationship.'

The phone went quiet, and Loretta had to check Ethan was still there. He thanked her for calling and felt some comfort that she could still work with him in future.

'I don't believe it,' Ethan said. 'Mum's, like, two miles away.'

'So what? She obviously doesn't care about us. And how can she know for sure? I bet she hasn't seen her for real. I bet she read that off a computer. Don't get your hopes up.'

Ethan doubted the information too, but Loretta was so certain. Within a minute a text message came through from Loretta with the full address, not that they needed it, everyone knew the Ubley Estate. You couldn't miss the massive sandstone property on the hill which looked over the city.

Just this news alone got Ethan onto his feet and made him pace around. It was as if the call charged him, and the sparkle of the city carried across the street into his blood.

'What's got into you?' Heston said.

'Well for all the shit which has happened tonight, I suddenly feel a lot better. At last, I know what's been happening to me, and now I know where mum is. What's not to feel good about? So, I'm not bailing out. I'm skating this damn rail, and not for show either. I'm going to blow it up.'

## 16

## CRISPY BACON

The following morning, Chris rang Ethan's doorbell and wasn't prepared for the stranger behind the door. Ethan had a bright red t-shirt on and khaki cargos.

'Jesus. What's happened to you?' Chris hadn't seen him wearing anything other than black before. He rolled his camera bag in and knocked it into the leg of the dining room table.

'Want some breakfast?' Ethan carried across the plates and set them down on the table.

'Nice place you've got here.'

'My brother helped out with it.' Ethan pushed a bag of white bread across the table. 'Come on. Tuck in.'

'Who turned you into a housewife overnight? Are you ill or something?'

'Nope. I'm happy.' Ethan cut into a sausage and

dipped it in tomato sauce. 'After you left last night, I found out Heston had been sabotaging my edits. Or attempting to. But, anyway, once I slapped him about a bit it turned out to be a good night. I've never slept so well.' He told Chris what happened with more clarity than ever before. It was as if his brain wired everything up in his sleep to make perfect sense. He knew how to handle N27, how to deal with his old crew, and how to tackle the filming later that night. He felt as if he had punched himself out on the curb, and a new self had emerged. Chris listened between bites of bacon, as one thought blended into the next. Chris let him get it all out until the final mention of the retail rail.

'Tonight, we're filming in the Hives Honey building.'

Chris almost spat out his beans. 'We're doing what? How?' He put down his knife and fork. 'I'm not breaking in!'

'We won't have to. The door locks are dodgy, and the alarm isn't activated.'

Chris stabbed a piece of Ethan's stupidity with a fork and chewed on it slowly. 'You *are* breaking in?'

'No. It's open. I just told you.'

'It doesn't matter if the door is wide open. It's still breaking in.'

'We used to *break-in* all the time. It's called: skating, or have you forgotten?'

'We used to jump fences, which isn't the same. Have you forgotten I'm trying to get into Uni?'

'You won't get into trouble. We've been through this before. There's no chance of it. You'll get a slap on the wrist at most.' Ethan shoved a fried egg into his mouth and swallowed it whole. He then realised Chris was giving him a funny look. 'What?'

'I still don't get why we're going to all this trouble,' Chris said. 'Who are you trying to impress? Now you know that your brother has been making things difficult for you, and he's told you what you need to do to get out of your contract, why bother? Follow his plan, create a mediocre edit, let the stats keep falling so they no longer need you.'

'You don't get it. This is more than just an upload to the Internet. I've got a show. I'm a public figure with responsibilities. Then there's the kids, who look up to me. They're stoked to watch each new edit. I don't want to let them down.'

Chris had stopped eating.

'What are you looking at me like that for?'

'This is all about you,' Chris said. 'I know you had a shitty upbringing, but can't you get your hugs somewhere else?'

'It's not like that. I want to do a good job, that's all.'

'No, you aren't,' Chris stressed. 'This is about impressing those kids, who've got a billion other videos to watch by the way. This is ridiculous.

You're going to put your life on the line, and mine, risk losing your job, and maybe get everyone a criminal record. All to impress some skateboarders.'

'You're so wrong.'

Chris was flat-out wrong. Ethan was almost sure of it. 'I'm doing this to help you too, remember?' He said, 'I didn't have to pick you. I could've picked any one of the other skaters. This isn't about me. This is about the scene. The skaters. The footage.'

'This is *all* about your *ego*,' Chris stated.

'No, it isn't.' But the word *ego* settled in his head. It couldn't be all about him, there was everyone else involved in the edits, too. He was certain, but the same questions kept popping up: was it really about him? Chris kept coming up with more and more examples of *Ethan first, and everyone else second*. And he had a lot of examples as if he'd memorised them.

At the end of Chris' rant, Ethan felt deflated.

'I didn't realise,' he finally admitted. 'Maybe you're right.' He slumped and covered his mouth with his hands. After a few seconds, he leant forward and rubbed his face as if he'd risen out from a pool of water. The choices he'd been making, all the efforts he had been taking to build up these edits were tangled up into what he really needed and wanted. Then that phrase came to mind again. *His Slings and Arrows.*

'Hello, hello. Anybody home?' Chris waved in front of Ethan's face until he blinked back into life.

'Do you need CPR or is your heart going to pump some blood back into your face?'

Ethan couldn't stop thinking about his brother's words last night. 'Heston was right. It's all about me.'

'No. I said that.'

Everything began to come together again. He didn't need to thump those puzzle pieces into position anymore. The picture built itself and he didn't like it.

'How can I fix this?'

'Stop doing stupid shit?'

'Then let's start tonight. No-one wants me to do that rail, so I won't. What do I care?'

'Uh, wait.' Chris felt a week's wages vanish from his bank account. 'We've just gone to all that trouble to set it up. You can't back out now. Let's not get into some depressive stupor. We can still do this.'

'You've just spent ten minutes trying to talk me out of it.'

'No. I've been telling you…'

'Besides, I didn't think you wanted to do it anyway?'

Chris felt the back of his head as if he'd been whacked with his own idea. 'Well, I suppose it could be fun.'

## 17

## DESK RAMP RUN

It was midnight on a cold, dry evening when taxi headlights shone across a small gathering of trees and caught a glimpse of two figures sat against the trunks. They had been there for nearly an hour, watching people meander through the streets, waiting for the right moment to move. The pair timed security guards walking around the premises, and noticed it always happened the same way: a single guard would leave via the front exit, light a cigarette, look briefly up and down the street, and set off around the building with a walkie-talkie in one hand and a torch in the other. Ethan had broken into places like this a thousand times before and knew this one was easy.

Chris, however, nibbled the skin on the side of his fingers.

It took about forty-five minutes for the guard to

complete his loop and walk around the back towards the bays.

'It's time to go.' Ethan set off across the street with Chris close behind.

'About time. My legs were almost asleep.'

They followed the guard around the side of the building and watched him go in through the fire door.

'How are we getting in exactly?' Chris whispered.

'I've had a grand tour by the owner, and he told me the fire exit doors jam when closed. So, I know *that*.' Ethan pointed at the door the guard walked through, 'isn't as shut as it looks.' When the coast was clear, they both ran to the door and Ethan gave a gentle tug on the handle. It popped open. 'See. No crime committed.'

'Oh, perfect,' Chris said. 'Also, let's help ourselves to some cash from the till. What about the alarms?'

'They're all disabled until the doors are fixed.'


Ethan pulled the fire door gently shut and listened for the sound of the guard's footsteps. He was a corridor ahead of them. Once he'd passed through into the next, they ran to a hiding spot: a doorway, a filing cabinet, or desk. As they passed through each set of doors, Ethan wedged half a laundry peg underneath. It was a tip he learnt from Dixel, who told him that the way *in*to a location could be as slow and as considered as she liked, but just sometimes the exit needed to be fast.

The acrylic coated concrete flooring reflected the ceiling lights in its polished surface. They had to walk carefully to prevent their shoes from squeaking and both were desperate to throw down their boards and skate.

At the turn of a corner, the guard went into an office: his base for the night. The tinny sound of a football match from a radio came from the room and cut off when the door closed. A glance through the door's small porthole window showed a desk stacked with CCTV monitors and two guards playing cards.

'We need to make sure they stay in there.' Ethan whispered. Blocking the door wouldn't keep the guards trapped forever, but anything to slow them down would help. Chris wheeled across a filing cabinet and positioned it under the handle. Now it couldn't drop any more than a centimetre before it hit steel. Ethan locked the cabinet's wheels in place.

'We've got about an hour before the guard does another loop.'

It was time to find something to skate and they didn't have to look hard. The long corridors were empty apart from the occasional pot plant and bench seats. Once they found a spot far enough away from the guards' office, they dragged a bench, which was the perfect height to flip over, out into the middle of the aisle. A bit further down, the aisle widened into an open-plan office. They cleared a desk of its telephone, computer, monitor, and paperwork, and slid it out alongside a second. The conjoined tables gave them a four-metre-long ledge to ride along and ollie off. All they needed was a ramp of some sort. The warehouse area had exactly what they needed: a sheet of aluminium loading bay ramp designed to wheel pallets on and off the back of lorries. It was perfect. Ethan carried it out and set it on top of some pallet blocks to create a kicker. Chris went to the end of the corridor and jammed the door open with more pegs. They now had a clear path through into reception.

Ethan practised a few kickflips, nollie-flips, and nollie-heels to get warmed up and ollied a few times over the bench. He then took a test run over the obstacles with a frontside 180, a half-cab, a little nose-bump, and a kickflip. He ollied off the kicker onto the desk and three-flipped off onto the floor.

The line felt good, but he needed something else. They went back into the warehouse and scouted around until they found an old grey plastic 26-inch Toshiba TV. Ethan wiped the dust off the curved glass screen.

'I can't believe people used to own these things.' A satisfying plastic click sounded with each button press. 'And it's only got five channels.' Chris wheeled it back on his board and they lifted it onto the desk.

Ethan gave it a shake.

'I bet it'll move as soon as you hit it.'

'I'll only hit it once. It'll be fine.'

Chris took out his camera turned it on, checked the settings, and put on his wide-angle. 'I'm ready to go.'

Ethan skated to the end of the corridor.

Chris hit record.

With two quick pushes, Ethan set off. He kick-flipped, then nollie-180-flipped to get around to fakie ready for the fast-approaching bench. He backside switch-flipped over it and landed clean with enough time to get one good push in before hitting the aluminium ramp. He ollied onto the desk, set his feet, and tre-flipped off the end. After another couple of pushes, he frontside flipped and power slid to a stop before he reached the reception area.

'Let me know when you want me to light the rail.' Chris pulled out the little bottle of lighter fluid from his pocket.

'Not yet. We need more footage first.'

The friends went back to the beginning of the corridor and found another line: a nollie-heel followed by a switch back-heel, then a kickflip over the bench, a switch 180 ollie off the kicker onto the desk to get himself facing forward, and an impossible off onto the floor. He pushed on with Chris following close behind and ended on a tre-flip.

'Get that?'

Chris had.

'Go again?'

'Yeah. I'm starting to get warmed up now.'

Again, the friends set off this time doing the whole run in reverse. Ethan switch-flipped on the flat and ollied up into a frontside noseslide on the edge of the desk. The laminated wood surface slid nicely to fakie, which led to a full-cab over the bench and ended on a final switch-flip.

The tricks came easy and with plenty of footage banked, the evening would soon be in the bag.

'Another line?' Chris was ready to go, so Ethan started with a quick run and threw his board down. Chris pushed hard to catch up and filmed a 360 shove-it on the flat, a nose bump over the bench, a nose-wheelie cross the desks, and a nollie-heel off onto the flat. However, before Ethan landed, he heard Chris' foot squeak across the floor as he forced himself to stop. Up ahead, a security guard stood at the end of the corridor.

A voice bellowed down the corridor. 'Hold it right there!'

They looked at each other, grabbed their bags, and ran in the opposite direction.

## 18

## BREAKING THROUGH

The two friends sprinted through the hallway, around a corner, bashing into office chairs and falling through the doors into another room. Chris slid out on a sharp left and knocked himself into a table. Once Ethan checked he was okay, they raced off again. The corridors went on forever, and the guard relentlessly chased them despite it being far more effort than his pay grade required. The pair ran through a laboratory, knowing it would only be a matter of time before they hit a locked door, and when it arrived, Ethan felt it. The thud bounced him back off this wooden wall knocking the wind out of him.

Ethan groaned and felt his ribs whilst trying to pat his pockets down. 'Where's the door pass?'

'The last place I saw it was back by the desks,'

Chris said. 'You said you couldn't skate with stuff in your pockets. Didn't you pick it up?'

'Of course, I didn't. Otherwise, I wouldn't be asking you for it, would I?'

'Don't get shitty with me. I'm not the dumb-ass here.'

The dead-end had trapped them and the guard was only seconds away. Hiding was their only option. Chris hid behind a desk and Ethan found his own. The guard entered the room and sprinted through but as he passed, Ethan stuck his foot out. The guard tripped and slammed headfirst into the door, then slumped to the ground. The room went quiet.

'Is he dead?' Chris asked.

'I doubt it.'

'You're making a habit of sweeping people's legs.'

'It seems to work.' Ethan nudged the unconscious guard with his foot.

'So, what now?'

A second guard entered the opposite end of the room. Ethan grabbed the sleeping guard's door pass and held it up to the panel. The light changed from red to green, buzzed, and unlocked.

'Which way's out?' Chris' voice sounded as though he was twelve.

As far as Ethan was concerned this running was wasted energy when he could be skating. At least now he had a door pass, things were looking up again. He grabbed a chair and jammed it underneath the door handle. 'This way.'

'I'm pretty sure it's this way,' Chris said.

'You don't know that. You've got no idea. This building goes on forever and I've been inside it before. Trust me.'

Chris hesitated, clearly not convinced. That Uni course must have bubbled up in his thoughts again, seeing his application slip away with each minute of being stuck inside. Going right didn't feel good; he still wanted to go left. 'You go that way,' Chris said. The guard thumped on the door trying to break through it. 'I'm going this way.'

Ethan didn't have the energy to argue with Chris. 'I have the door pass, you idiot.'

'I can't keep running further into this place. Why aren't we doubling back? We jammed the doors open with pegs.' It was actually a reasonable idea, but Ethan couldn't go back. He didn't like having Chris slow him up and saw it as a good opportunity to go it alone. He remembered Chris shaking that little bottle of lighter fluid: someone needed to be ready for filming.

'Okay but take my board with you. I'm not going to need it. When you get outside, watch the entrance. When you see me, fire up the rail, and have your camera ready.'

Chris nodded.

Ethan noticed that the guard had stopped thumping on the doors. 'Where have you gone?' He looked through the little window but couldn't see him. Then he heard the guard approaching from another direction: he'd found another route. Chris hid in one of the side rooms and Ethan ran into another and got a third of the way in, when he saw the first guard, cupping the lump on his head through a door window. Ethan hit the lights and plunged the place into darkness, until a few seconds later when the guard's torchlight flicked on. It gave him a fraction more time to get some distance on the guard and let Chris disappear in the other direction.

Whether through sheer luck or natural GPS, Ethan reached an area he recognised: the room with the wall of bees. Deep brown waves from this hypnotic texture shifted behind the glass which made focusing on it difficult. It felt alien. He held the pass up to the door, waited for it to unlock, and pushed the handle with a clammy hand and pictured his death by a million bee stings.

The corridor was black as beetle legs, but there were no bees. Beyond the ceiling and walls, the hum and buzz of forty-thousand bees shook his nerves. It was as if he'd entered an engine room of a huge vehicle. The skin on the back of his head tightened and urged him on. He fumbled with his pass at the second door as the guard opened the first. Ethan pushed through into a powerful white light. He covered his eyes, slammed the door again, and fell to the floor.

## 19

## POLLINATION

As he pulled his hands away, he saw plants, lots of them, enough to fill a garden centre. At first, he thought he was dreaming, and rubbed his eyes some more. These plants were uniform, and tightly packed, growing up towards this indoor greenhouse sky of bright lights. It was obvious that bees needed plants, so a garden made sense, but this was no freshly mown lawn with decorative flower beds. This was waist-high, industrial, a tennis court wide, and two aces deep. He was no gardener but easily recognised thousands of marijuana plants.

'Oh my God.' He remembered Royston saying there were more bees behind that wall. 'No wonder you didn't want me back here.'

A security guard thumped on the door from behind.

He brushed his hands over the plants and tried

to see how far back the room went. There must have been hundreds of thousands of pounds worth. Hives must have been supplying all of the South with a crop of that size. So much for the honey business. No-wonder no-one ever saw anyone buying the stuff. Royston was just another dealer.

The door buzzed and the panel flashed from red to green. Ethan watched the lock spin open, and with nowhere to run, he jumped into the plants.

The guards bundled into the room, and he heard the door slam shut. He crawled on and hoped they hadn't noticed the plants parting. They began searching the room and Ethan kept crawling.

When he'd got far enough in the field, he stopped. Once they'd finish searching the perimeter, they'd know he was inside it. He desperately wanted to pluck a few buds and shove them in his pocket. He took a right turn and made his way to the edge of the crop. A pair of black trousers and polished steel toe-capped boots passed him heading towards the back. When it was clear, he crawled out. This was a good idea until he was out in the open, clueless, with no real plan for escape. He quietly ran towards the back corner of the room, all the while looking for an exit, an office window, or anything helpful. From the bottom corner of the crops, he saw the two guards in the opposite corner searching the edge of the plants for any sign of the intruder.

A guard looked back up the line and saw him. Ethan pulled back out of view, but it was too late. He sprinted back up to the front of the building, as the guards shouted after him. They only had half the distance to cover and within seconds he'd be in full view.

Something brushed his side. It was a bee suit attached to the wall. Next to it appeared to be a hatch release button. For what, he didn't know, but he was out of options. Before he had time to think he already had two legs into the suit and zipped up the front. A guard had reached the top of the crop and was only a few metres away.

He smacked the hatch release button.

The guard skidded to a halt. 'No, no, no,' he shouted.

A vented section in the ceiling opened and the hum and blur of bees made their way through a shaft. Within a couple of seconds, they had begun pouring into the room. Thousands upon thousands of them spiralled around in the air and pitched on everything they could. Gathering in the creases of the ceiling and dotted around all over the walls.

Ethan yanked up the zip on his chest and flipped the helmet over his head. As the bees pitched on his face guard, he recoiled in automatic panic for a moment until he calmed himself down.

One of the guards whipped his arms around blindly trying to bat them away with his torch, whilst the other was half in the second suit trying to zip it up.

Ethan couldn't wait around and needed to get out of there. He unlocked the door and went through, some bees followed, but not enough to worry him. This door needed the pass again, so he unzipped his suit down to his waist to reach his pocket. The guard was already close behind, as he yanked on the door handle, and slammed his door shut. Ethan kicked the suit off his legs. Chris was waiting, camera in hand and Ethan's board in the other.

'Are you ready to go?'

## 20

## BLASTED

A guard got out through the bee room door and shouted at them to stop, but Ethan had already started pushing. Chris kept up alongside and held the camera low and close. Through the plate-glass windows, Ethan saw the rail up ahead and hoped Chris hadn't forgotten to pour the lighter fluid all over it. Ethan kickflipped up the couple of steps out through the reception door and only had enough time for one push before ollieing up onto the rail.

His front truck landed perfectly and hit the strike switch. In a tenth of a second, the flame shot out from under him and covered the full length of the rail. Chris panned out wide. As the end approached, Ethan realised he was nose-heavy and wasn't going to be able to manual off like Bryon wanted. He braced himself and knew it was too late to worry about that extra explosive packed into the rail.

He felt the small click of his truck ride over the trigger mechanism, then shut his eyes and held his breath. There was no way he was going to waste everyone's time with a bail.

A huge explosion of light and plasterboard blew out from underneath him. First, he felt the whoosh of the blast, fragments of something hitting his face, then the fiery heat. Despite trying to stay on and predict when the floor would arrive, the blast was too much. The board touched down, but he was thrown forward in a mess of debris. A wave of draft and heat singed every exposed hair on his body as he rolled along, disorientated, and desperate to get further from whatever was behind him. When he came to a rest in a ball, chunks of block and board all tumbled around. His ears rang. His mouth was full of dust, and he had no idea how much damage the blast had done. His legs were still attached. That was good enough. Any other injury he could deal with.

As the dust storm cleared, he rolled over and saw the security guards on their backs like fat beetles by the doors. Chris appeared out of nowhere holding his head from a concussion. They were both okay, except for that damn ringing in his ears. He grabbed his board and got up slowly with Chris' help.

Behind them, a vehicle's tyres screeched along the curb. It was Bryon's van. The rear side door slid open. 'Get in,' he shouted.

They staggered across the pavement and fell inside. The door slammed shut and the van sped off as fast as it arrived. It felt like they were in a getaway car, as everyone had to grip something solid to stop being thrown into each other. On the straight roads, Chris tried to clear the crap from his ears, whilst Ethan shook the plasterboard from his clothes.

'I told you it was too much,' Bryon said.

Ethan rocked his jaw from side to side and jammed one finger in his ear. 'Did you get it, Chris?'

Chris spooled through the footage until the closing shot. It was perfectly framed with Ethan's wheels filling the screen until the final ollie. There were only three seconds of him on the rail, as it caught alight, and blasted out from under him before he'd even landed. The screen went completely white, then black and white again filled with static, whilst the audio crackled as Chris tumbled from his board. When the picture settled and the smoke cleared, they saw Ethan slowly moving on the ground.

'Yes!' Ethan shouted and hit the camper roof with his hand. 'It doesn't get better than that.'

The footage was incredible. If Chris had been a

metre closer, they wouldn't have caught the blast on film. Everyone gathered around the little screen and watched the rewind again. For a moment the joy wiped away all of Ethan's worries and stresses. The danger and panic of the guards, his fears of failure, the pressure of producing another edit for the week. Everything lifted. Any other footage of him slamming on a trick would have been thrown away, but this was golden. It was the perfect end to an edit he needed. Better still everyone was OK. No-one hung around to check on the guards, but they'd eventually wonder what the hell hit them.

'So much for Hives Honey being legit.' The others had no idea what else Ethan had seen. 'I found a field of marijuana plants growing as tall as my chest inside. The honey is just a front. They're growing weed, and either processing it into the honey, distributing it, or both. Hives is a crook.'

The van took a hard left and knocked everyone into each other.

'Ease up, Lewis Hamilton!'

Ethan suddenly realised that someone else was driving.

Bryon leant forward and tapped the driver on the shoulder. 'Have you met Chris before?'

The driver appeared briefly in the mirror before glancing back at the road. Ethan recognised the eyes but wasn't sure who it was until he she spoke.

'Pleased to meet you, Chris,' Dixel shouted into

the back. 'I'm also a filmer for N27, but for some reason, I wasn't invited to this party.'

Chris said *Hi*, whilst Ethan looked at Bryon and tried to think of something fast. 'Hey, I'm sorry,' he finally blurted.

Dixel took a fast right and everybody bashed into each other again.

'I think you can slow down now,' Bryon said.

'I wanted to tell you, but I couldn't.'

'Tell me what? How you didn't want to work with me? Thanks.' Another sharp turn threw everyone left and Ethan whacked his head on the window post.

'I was trying to find out who had been screwing with my locations. So, I couldn't tell anybody.'

'Right.' She wasn't buying it. 'Well, you managed to tell these two.'

More apologies flowed thick and fast, but the damage was done.

'It was nothing personal,' he said. 'For what it's worth, I really missed hanging with you. You're the best filmer.'

'Uh,' Chris said.

'No offence.'

## 21

**RESPITE**

A ping-pong of quips and apologies continued, which bored Bryon. 'So, what are you going to do now?'

'For starters,' Ethan said. 'I'm taking control of the locations. N27 wants to brush me under the carpet, but I'm not playing that game. Just the opposite. I'm going to do a killer job.'

'But they could dump you after this mess you've created.'

'No chance of that.' Ethan pulled the Ubley Ogre leaflet out of his pocket and held it up for Bryon and Chris. 'They've got a new promotion planned for me.'

Chris took the leaflet for a closer look. 'Oh, this is bad.'

'N27s precious new sponsor is a drug baron.

I've seen his entire production, and I'm happy to broadcast it if he gets in my way.'



By the next day, Ethan's anger at N27 had passed and he couldn't wait to throw a crappy location back at them if it wasn't good enough. Not even Heston would argue against him now everything was out in the open.

Eric from maintenance was in his usual seat in reception. 'You look surprisingly happy, considering,' he said.

'What have I got to feel bad about?' Ethan replied. 'And considering what?' But before Eric could say anything, he had a blockage in the gents that needed dealing with. Wendy from Marketing rushed out of an office and apologised. Ethan figured that everyone must have heard about the rail explosion—bad news travels fast—but then they probably hadn't seen the footage yet. Ethan's stars aligned even further that morning, as Wendy confirmed that the Ubley Ogre event was under review. *Cancelled*, was the word Ethan was looking for, but until then, a fat red pen hovering over it was good enough. Besides, with the info he now had on Hives Honey, there was no way he was going to let that reputation killer go ahead.

Wendy's next meeting was about to begin, and

as she stepped through the door, Ethan briefly saw Royston Hives at the table. *What the hell was he doing there?*

Dixel stepped out of the meeting room to his left and yanked him inside. 'Have you heard the news?' she said. 'Your edit has been pulled.'

'Why?'

'Probably because you blew up the front of a business and injured two security guards, you moron. Why do you think? You've been replaced with Ricard's Line-life.'

'Again?' And just like that Ethan felt the sideways push of N27 just as Heston said they would. There was no way he was going to give in without one final bang at least.

'Apparently, they pulled it because of an *editorial decision based on public endangerment and criminal damage* if you can believe that.'

Ethan thanked her for the heads up, then realised spending another minute in the building was a complete waste of time. The only thing which prevented him leaving was a police car pulling into a parking space outside.

He knew it was for him, but he couldn't let the morning go this way. He needed a private word with Blacker to apply some pressure on Royston. And that wasn't going to work with police in the building.

*Shit.*

Two officers, one male, one female, walked into reception and asked for his name. A frosted glass wall hid him as they walked through the hall towards Blacker's office. He greeted them, but the offer of a handshake and coffee was politely declined. This wasn't social. Everyone sat. Within seconds, a pig wrapped in the curtain cloth of Royston Hives appeared at Blacker's door and invited himself in. He huffed like he was late for the meeting and pulled up a chair. The look on Blacker's face confirmed it was a surprise to him too, but the officers took out their notebooks as if new information had arrived. Royston blustered his way onto the agenda, raising his palms to the ceiling, and bouncing a joke around the room. It was the type of joke which could only lift the corner of Blacker's mouth, as he slipped a sideways glance at the officers. They wrote a lot of things down and appeared to double-check with the boss.

'I think he's covering up what happened,' Dixel said.

'The last thing he wants is an investigation.'

Within minutes, the officers stood and put away their notebooks as if they had better things to attend to. Blacker walked them out and left Royston filling the doorway with swollen relief.

'He doesn't look happy,' Dixel said. 'I don't think you'll want to run into him for a while.'

## 22

## A LONG DRIVE RIDE

The walk up to the sandstone Ubley Estate manor house on a cold autumn morning felt about as enjoyable as speaking at a Council meeting. Its sagging bay window eyes and dark wooden door looked down at him. Even Scottish highland cattle in the fields monitored this intruder with a disapproving snort.

Heston had no time for his *mother*, knowing she was so close and unwilling to make contact. It was down to Ethan to carry two fist-sized questions in his pockets: what happened, and why haven't you contacted us? Secretly he wanted a *Welcome Home* hug, but with each step that Ask was beginning to feel like a thin and painful splinter.

A vehicle rumbled over the cattle grid behind him, and he remembered how the house was recently sold. He didn't want to get into a conversation with the new owner, so he threw himself into the hedge. A dirty old Land Rover sped past, and he caught the briefest glimpse of a young, bearded man in a white shirt and a flat cap in the driver's seat. It could have been the owner, but the uncertainty added another question to his growing list. What was the connection with his mother? Was she renting there? Or living, like, with a boyfriend?

No sooner had he climbed out of the hedge and started walking up the drive again, a second vehicle rattled over the cattle grid. This time it was a red postal van. A hedge wouldn't be needed this time. The driver eased up beside him.

'Do you want a lift?' the driver asked. Ethan didn't, but the man had already opened the door.

'Thought I'd save you the long walk.'

He slammed it into gear as if it needed a thump and continued up the drive. Ethan wasn't in the mood for small talk but acknowledged a comment on the weather before returning to the trees flicking past his window.

When the van stopped at the house, the driver hopped out, grabbed his parcels, and went to the front door. The side door opened and the man from the Land Rover took in the parcels. It was only then that Ethan got out and thanked the mailman. After the post van had driven away down the drive, Ethan made a detour for the side door.

It was the entrance to the rear gardens and

there was a lot of it. Well maintained flowerbeds, a miniature maze of low clipped hedges patterned out ahead of him, small trees lined the paths and ivy covered the exterior walls. A wall of garden peas climbed fine green plastic netting that shielded him from the main house.

A hand landed on his shoulder and spun him around.

'Can I help you?'

It was the Land Rover driver.

'Me? Who the hell are you?' This sounded better in his head, and it should have stayed there. However, the man wasn't fazed by Ethan's jumble of words. 'Do you live here?'

'No. I'm the gardener. Are you looking for someone?'

The question was direct and heavy, and he should have been ready for it. The place was fancy. Too fancy for him to be there without good reason.

'I'm thinking about robbing the place.' This took a moment to sink in before the gardener started laughing. 'I'm, uh…' Ethan looked around the garden. 'I'm looking for some work.'

'Perfect. I take it you've seen one of the notes advertised?' The gardener walked on. 'Come on through. You don't look like the horticulturist type.'

'I do have green fingers sometimes. Evenings and weekends, mainly.'

'Great. Well, the owner isn't home yet, but if

you're happy to get your hands dirty, it'll increase your chances of getting hired.' The pair walked around to a long line of cuttings from a hedge. 'Clear all this over to the side of the house. You'll see a big pile ready for burning.'

The gardener left him to get on with it.

Ethan put on a pair of garden gloves, scooped up a handful branches and dropped them in the wheelbarrow. It was as good as empty. If they wanted to assume he was gardening, fine by him. He wanted an excuse to explore the house.

The first room he came across looked like the living room. It was full of dark heavy furniture and could have been a study. People with stupidly large sized houses tended to have too many rooms to know what to do with them. He could only see the back of a fair-haired woman was sat on a sofa leaning to one side as if reading a magazine.

*That could be her.*

He left the wheelbarrow, walked past the kitchen, and stepped inside the back door. Her voice echoed through the hallway, discussing an event, then the talking stopped. Ethan quickly looked for somewhere to hide, then she sneezed three short fast bursts. It was his mum. Him and Heston used to make finger guns and shoot each other whenever she did it. Bang, bang, bang!

He was relieved, annoyed, and shocked all at once, but it wasn't until he heard her tele-*phoney* voice that his skin began to prickle with fucks. Here she was, happy and healthy, living well, with no concern for her kids.

Loretta was right.

It must've been ten years since he had seen her. What had she been doing all this time?

In the hallway was an umbrella in a stand and a pair of shoes, a dog lead and some unopened mail. A letter with the name Catherine Hives on it. Which was weird because that was the same surname of Royston Hives. He suddenly remembered the news article of a local entrepreneur who bought the place and wished he'd paid more attention to it. But her name and his? *They'd married?* His *Slings and Arrows* lined up in his head and pushed any hope of joy out of his brain for the day. Everything was crumbling around him again. He didn't want to be there, see her, or ask anything. Those questions could be answered another time when he could think clearer.

A second voice came from the room: it was the gardener.

'Come on in,' he said. 'What did you say your name was?'

The gardener waved him into the room in that dumb friendly way of his. His mother looked at him but said nothing. She just raised her eyebrows like a dog who'd heard the word *biscuit*.

No-one spoke.

The gardener repeated his question.

*She knows my name. Say it.*

She just looked back at the gardener, like Ethan had learning difficulties. Even the gardener looked flustered as if he was using the wrong language.

'My. Name's. Matt.'

*Staccato* Matt. He felt as if he was eight again.

'Okay. Great. Matt. Right.'

'This is the lady of the house, Mrs Hives. She's got a quick chore for you. Let me know if there's anything you need. I'll be just outside.'

Ethan was suddenly alone with her.

'OK. Follow me,' she said.

Ethan couldn't take his eyes off her. The last time he saw her she was strapped to a gurney being wheeled out into an ambulance. Now, she was older and heavier, but even the thick makeup couldn't hide those eyes. He couldn't believe she didn't recognise him. Had he changed that much?

He followed her upstairs into a boy's bedroom.

'That suitcase.' She pointed to a large black plastic case on top of the wardrobe. 'I need it down.'

For a moment he felt invisible like a member of her staff. He wanted to grab her by the shoulders and shout in her face who he was. Then he felt stupid whilst she waited, so he lifted the suitcase down and placed it on the bed. The room had everything you'd find in young man's bedroom: an

XBOX, clothes thrown over a chair, a laptop, some photos pinned to the wall, socks were strewn around, and a wastebasket full of crumpled paper.

'Is this your son's room?' The empty words fell out of his mouth. He wanted to know, who was living there with her.

'It's my stepson's,' she said. 'My children are all grown up, doing their own thing.'

He bit his tongue. 'They live with their dad?' The question tightened his brain, shrivelling it into a walnut.

She dismissed the thought with a wave of her hand. 'Oh, no. He's probably in a gutter somewhere.'

That was the final stomach punch he couldn't handle. Family didn't matter, he didn't matter, his father didn't matter. It didn't make sense. He knew his stepfather was an alcoholic like her. She must've been on about his real dad. For a moment, he just looked at her, hoping that she would recognise him.

'What are you looking at? That'll be all. You can go back to the garden work now.'

*What a bitch.* Her drugged up past could have affected her memory, but he dismissed it quickly. He didn't want to make excuses. Hating her was much easier.

Heavy steps thumped onto the doormat from the kitchen and a loud, booming voice announced he was home. Ethan recognised Royston instantly, and that was his cue to leave. He made his way down the stairs quickly and shot out of the front door without even looking around for the Drug Lord of the Manor. He heard his mother say he'd just missed the new handyman.

'I haven't hired a handyman.'

# BOOK 5: NUTBAR DIY SAMPLE

# 1

## DITCH SPOT

Ethan's burnt orange T-shirt matched the biscuit tanned skin of Simon, the Marketing Director, who wanted him to skate down a slope. Simon was from London, and celebrated his new job at N27 with a status update. He was a doer, who meant business, but he also ate Haribo in his Vauxhall Insignia during lunch. Simon jogged up the hill as if what he had to say was important.

'Okay, guys.' He also liked to clap which he learnt on team-building camp. 'Let's just run through this again. All I need you to do is roll down the hill, arms wide…' He'd planned everything out during a long pub-lunch with an iPad and a pencil balanced on his top lip. '… and skate down past us. Got it?' Thumbs went up like they were spring loaded.

Local grommets had gathered at the bottom of the flyover and were restless whilst waiting for some action. Who could blame them? They'd seen nothing but dumb stuff all afternoon.

The filming was for a series of promotional segments between programmes, except Simon had a funny idea of what skateboarding looked like. Ethan would have been fine filming those segments solo, but for some reason, a second skateboarder was needed and the first available freelancer was Elliott Sommers. And the last person on earth he wanted to be working with was Ethan.

'This is what you do all day?' Elliott hissed.

'Sometimes,' Ethan sighed.

'And there's me thinking you had a sweet job. I couldn't have been more wrong. I'm only here for the money, so don't go thinking we're friends again.'

A siren from a fire appliance slid through the air a mile down the hill. The truck popped out between trees and blinked its blue lights, racing to free a cow from a ditch or rescue a cat from a tree. This morning's breaking news story announced a theft from a chemical distribution centre. Details were still being discovered, but the media behaved as if it was the crime of the century.

Simon noticed Ethan's elbow pads were on the floor.

'They're not needed. We're professionals.'

'You're also role models on national TV.' Simon handed them back and took up his position beside the cameraman again. Ethan put the pads back on as the muppet wasn't worth the battle.

Elliott was still complaining.

'We both agreed to do this,' Ethan said to him. 'So, let's just get it done, then we can get back to some proper skating.'

'*I'll* be proper skating,' Elliott scoffed. '*This* is *your* world, not mine.' That tone was supposed to hurt, but the comment just hung in the air between them, all stained and stinking of Elliott's intensions.

'You can't keep blaming me for a company which would have gone bust anyway.'

'You don't know that,' Elliott said. 'It's so ironic that the biggest loser on the team ended up with the cushy job.'

Simon waved his sheet of paper at the bottom of the slope, and they set off again. He mirrored their entire routine out of frame like a primary school teacher guiding a nativity play. He held his arms wide, faked a wobble, and tried to encourage Ethan to raise his arms, whilst they skidded on their tails, flashed teeth at each other, high-fived, and rolled the rest of the way down the hill.

'Great. That was just perfect.' Simon trotted after them. 'But this time, when you look at each other, really put your heart into it. You're doing what you love, yeah?' Simon clapped his happiness out as they walked back up the hill.

'With any luck, they'll edit me out completely,' Elliott said.

They got back into positions and Simon pointed to Ethan's elbows. Those pads had slipped off again.

The next attempt was only marginally better than the previous, but after bombing the hill Ethan kicked out a powerslide and just missed Simon's ankles.

Simon jumped back out of the way, but Ethan was too far down the hill to hear the abuse thrown at him.

A dark grey old Volvo pulled in under the flyover. Elliott's head dropped as he saw who it was, and his usual dumb sneer slid down to his Etnies. The car door jammed and Elliott's dad needed to kick it, then he struggled to get out of the seat like tall men do when they'd bought from a dealership with limited choice of vehicles. Thin, dirty fingers pulled his crumpled shirt straight and swept back his hair. It made no difference to his appearance.

'I just need a couple of minutes,' Elliott shouted.

'What do you want, boy?'

'I've got this business idea which can make a tonne of money. I've got everything here.' Elliott flashed his phone screen up too quick to get a proper look. 'I wanna buy some boards, but I need to borrow some money.'

His dad listened with a look which said *dumb-idea* and hitched his hands on his hips as if he knew where the story was going. 'How much?'

'I'll put it with the hundred and fifty I'll get from this job then pay you back a hundred a month.'

'How much!' His dad took the phone and squinted into the screen. He was humouring. Building up hope, lifting it high with possibilities where it caught the sun and looked pretty. The crash always killed if the fall was high enough. Ethan could see it, but Elliott couldn't or didn't want to.

'I wanna start a skate company. There's no decent shop for miles and the only choice we've got is run by an idiot. With this, I can buy in bulk, and sell to everyone at a profit. Easy money.'

'How much?!'

'Five-hundred.'

'And then we'll be business partners. How much do I get?'

'No. I mean, it'll just be me. A loan.'

'Then forget it. Get a proper job like everyone else does; one that pays real money.'

Elliott fell from six-stories to his death, right

there. His dad stepped over his son's corpse and climbed back into the car complaining about wasting his time. 'This,' he showed the racing section of the paper with biro blue circles marked. 'Lightning Blue, at 100 to 1. Now that's something worth putting five-hundred on.'

Hope stretched and snapped with that familiar sound of a car pulling away. Ethan made a mental note to ask, one day when things were good between them again, if his dad ever smacked him around too.

'Break time over.' Simon clapped his action-hands like he was directing a pantomime. He needed everyone to stay focused, be more skater-y, extreme, and a bit cooler.

'So, um,' Elliott hesitated. 'If any more jobs like this come up…'

'They pop-up occasionally, but I'll put your name forward.'

That ask hurt judging by the silence as they walked back up the hill.

'Are you really starting a company?'

'The industry isn't coming to me, is it?' Then he swore to himself at the shadow of suck his old man left behind. 'He's got the money. Five-hundred isn't a crazy amount.'

Ethan searched for the right thing to say but it must have looked like pity or something because Elliott took it the wrong way.

'I don't need your help,' Elliott said. 'I just need cash.'

Simon wanted them back up the hill to go again, but the grommets were ready to leave.

'I've a better idea,' Ethan shouted.

**OTHER TITLES**

Read the rest of the Ethan Wares Skateboard series now:

Book 1: The Blocks
Book 2: Abandoned
Book 3: Pool Staker
Book 5: Nutbar DIY

## AUTHOR'S NOTE

If you liked this story and would be interested in reading more, you can join my mailing list at https://skatefiction.co.uk and become one of my beta readers who get early access to new stories, give feedback, and receive reader copies in advance.

If you loved the book, please leave a positive review wherever you purchased it as this is the main way good books spread and help people discover me.

Thanks - Mark

## ABOUT THE AUTHOR

Mark Mapstone is a UK skateboarder, writer, and author of the Ethan Wares Skateboard Series books.

After discovering there were no fiction books written for skateboarders with realistic skateboarding in them, and being qualified with a degree in creative writing from the prestigious Bath Spa University, Mark decided he was perfectly positioned to cater this audience.

In-between road-trips, an infinite Instagram feed of videos to watch, and discovering bruises on himself which he has no-idea how they got there, Mark uses his knowledge of the current skateboarding world to create exciting and authentic stories which every skateboarder goes through daily.

Follow Mark on Instagram: @7plywood.

© 2021 Mark Mapstone

Published by Credible Ink Publishing

Forth edition

No part of this publication may be reproduced, stored or transmitted in any form or by any means, electronic, mechanical, photocopying, recording, scanning, or otherwise without written permission from the publisher. It is illegal to copy this book, post it to a website, or distribute it by any other means without permission. This novel is entirely a work of fiction. The names, characters and incidents portrayed in it are the work of the author's imagination. Any resemblance to actual persons, living or dead, events or localities is entirely coincidental. Mark Mapstone asserts the moral right to be identified as the author of this work.

All rights reserved.